Advance Praise for *Swans Don't Swim in a Sewer*

"Melissa's mom said, 'You can't give up; you just keep going…that's what Sheryl did for us.' Sheryl McCollum, my friend, is far more than an investigator; she's a champion for the voiceless and a guardian of untold narratives. With relentless determination, she unveiled the truth behind Melissa Wolfenbarger's disappearance, involving a shocking twist with Melissa's serial killer father. I am proud and inspired by her work; it's a testament to her skills and heart. Where others saw barriers, Sheryl found stepping stones."

—Susan Hendricks, former Weekend Express anchor, author, and podcaster

"The Melissa Wolfenbarger case needed a fresh set of eyes and didn't get an ordinary pair, it got Mac's! One investigator can make all the difference in a cold case and Sheryl 'Mac' McCollum is the best there is!"

—Sgt. Joseph Giacalone, (retired), NYPD, supervisor detective squad

"A tale full of twists and turns about a crime scene investigator leaving no stone unturned in the hunt for Melissa's killer…one such stone led to the mindset of a serial killer, which resulted in an unlikely yet masterful partnership between the cops and Melissa's father to catch her killer in one of Atlanta's notorious cold case murder mysteries."

—Scott Duffey, FBI, (retired), supervisory special agent

"A fascinating true Hannibal Lecter story in which Mac describes how an imprisoned Atlanta serial murderer, and his wife who had assisted him, helped her catch the murderer of their daughter."

—Michael M. Baden, MD, former chief medical examiner, New York City

“The Devil went down to Georgia and met his match in Sheryl McCollum. This harrowing yet captivating tale underscores the profound complexity of human psychology and the dark connections that sometimes emerge in the pursuit of truth.”

—Linda Kenney Baden, Esq., high-profile criminal attorney

“Some cases seemingly have no hope of being solved—no DNA, no eyewitnesses, nothing apparent that can be used to identify the offender. The victim’s mother has never given up hope, though waves of detectives have failed to solve her daughter’s brutal murder, and brings her case to Sheryl ‘Mac’ McCollum. Mac, initially out of compassion but then obsession, digs in and tries something no one else had—using a killer to catch a killer.”

—Paul Holes, *The New York Times* bestselling author, podcaster, and television host

"This story will pull at your heartstrings and make you re-think how a killer's mind works. McCollum's intuition and investigative drive takes you on a journey that is both intense and spellbinding. It's a story you will never forget."

—Aphrodite Jones, bestselling author of *Levi's Eyes.*

Swans Don't Swim in a Sewer

SOLVING THE COLD CASE OF THE FLINT RIVER KILLER'S DAUGHTER

SHERYL "MAC" McCOLLUM

A POST HILL PRESS BOOK
ISBN: 979-8-89565-282-4
ISBN (eBook): 979-8-89565-283-1

Swans Don't Swim in a Sewer:
Solving the Cold Case of the Flint River Killer's Daughter

Cover design by Conroy Accord

Post Hill Press
New York • Nashville
posthillpress.com

Published in the United States of America
2 3 4 5 6 7 8 9 10

For Melissa

Contents

Foreword 9
Prologue....10
A Note from the Author....12

Chapter 1: The Woman in the Bermuda Shorts 15
Chapter 2: Norma....19
Chapter 3: Where I Come From....23
Chapter 4: Carl: The Killer 28
Chapter 5: Melissa 32
Chapter 6: The Beginning or the End: 2003....38
Chapter 7: The Investigation Begins: The Background 41
Chapter 8: Carl and Norma's Arrest: The Connection 47
Chapter 9: Loyalty 51
Chapter 10: Gathering the Team and Walking the Scene 57
Chapter 11: Karyn Greer 62
Chapter 12: Trace....68
Chapter 13: The Best of the Best....77
Chapter 14: Letters from Carl....82
Chapter 15: Not On My Worst Enemy 93
Chapter 16: Zone 7 107
Chapter 17: Roadblocks, Obstacles, and Walls.... 112
Chapter 18: The Moniker Makes the Killer.... 116
Chapter 19: Pot Likker.... 127
Chapter 20: 5 Percent of the Time.... 130

Chapter 21: Contraband 132
Chapter 22: Breaking Hearts 138
Chapter 23: 8 x 10 141
Chapter 24: Check All Traps 146
Chapter 25: Your Own Zone 7 150
Chapter 26: Are We There Yet? 154
Chapter 27: Stolen Moments 159
Chapter 28: Diesel Therapy 163
Chapter 29: Hand to God Moments 167
Chapter 30: Settle the Score 173
Chapter 31: Upside, Down, and Backwards 177
Chapter 32: To Get Away with Murder 182
Chapter 33: Heat Waves and Boiling Points 187
Chapter 34: Cleaning the Barn 195
Chapter 35: The Call 201
Chapter 36: Plea Deals, Bond Hearings, and Jury Duty? 208
Chapter 37: He's Gone 212
Chapter 38: The Jury Has Spoken 218

Final Thought from a Friend 224
Appendix 225
Acknowledgments 245
About the Author 255

Foreword

SHERYL MCCOLLUM CONTINUES HER ANGELIC work to heal the persistent pains resulting from unsolved homicide cases.

Unsolved murder cases become a source for constant streams of emotion that pour to create a reservoir of tears and uncertainty, pooled from the hearts of victims' families.

The cold case investigator works tirelessly with great fortitude to dry the stream and drain that reservoir, exposing a new horizon of hope where the angels of justice bring the darkness of the past into the light of the present, getting the closure that loved ones yearn for.

Swans Don't Swim in a Sewer presents an intriguing story told by Sheryl McCollum, a talented and respected investigator who has earned an exemplary reputation through a purposeful and meaningful career in which she has worked under the most unique and difficult circumstances.

This fascinating narrative shapes and captures such work in a context I have never seen. This extraordinary book presents a controversy that frames a paradox of perspective: The bad bends toward the arc of the good in a world where judgment often trumps curiosity. This extraordinary case illustrates Sheryl's premier insight and expertise under extreme circumstances, where she works to gather evidence that will shed light on the darkness.

From John B. Edwards

Prologue

THE JURY DID NOT HEAR everything. They did not see everything. I will show you and tell you many things the jury did not see and hear.

There was probable cause for arrest. There was an indictment. There was no offer of a plea bargain. The prosecution believed they had enough. Sometimes the jury gets it right. Sometimes the jury gets it wrong. I believe this is one of those times the jury got it wrong.

Christopher Wolfenbarger was found not guilty of the murder of Melissa Wolfenbarger. This story is how I worked with Melissa's father, a serial killer, to solve her case. In law enforcement we consider a case solved once there is an arrest. This case was solved by arrest.

Christopher was the last person to see Melissa alive.

He changed his story about the last time they were together.

He got rid of all of her belongings right after she disappeared according to their daughter Christina.

He moved to South Georgia. Hard to believe he thought she was ever going to return if she could not find him.

He left their children behind.

Told his children he knew how to hide a body and get away with it.

Neither he nor his family ever looked for Melissa after it was clear she was missing.

After knowing she was murdered he never called police wanting answers or offering help in solving the case.

Told his mom's preacher he did it. He told the preacher how he did it. He told the preacher why he did it!

Had a history of abuse toward Melissa.

He was arrested for hitting her.

Melissa got a TPO against him.

Her remains were found across the street from where he worked at the time.

His boss at Action Glass thought he stole a circular saw—because he never returned it. Melissa was dismembered with a circular saw.

Detectives from different jurisdictions over different decades thought he did it.

I offered Christopher's attorney the opportunity to read the book before publishing: "Thank you for asking, I'll consider it. Who is the publisher?" was his only question. I never heard back from him. Then at the 11th hour he asked me to send him a copy. I did and explained that since he waited a month the book was at the publisher. I told him I would need any issues by November 11th in order to make in necessary changes. I was clear that if I did not hear from him, I would understand he had zero issues or concerns and move forward with publication. I never heard from him.

I stand by our work.

A Note from the Author

HOOKERS. DRUG DEALERS. PIMPS. THIEVES. Killers. These are the kind of people I often work with. They make up the sounds, the pulse, and the life of the streets.

Old cops and veteran detectives often talk about knowing the streets. But for me, it's the underbelly of the streets that's most important. The gutter that flows to the sewer. The sewer that flows like a river of intel and knowledge is all but hidden to the good people walking aboveground.

When you're searching for evil you gotta go where the devil plays. I gotta deal with people, all kinds of people. But the reality is the sewer sometimes has experts that I need. I gotta go into the sewer and let the current take me wherever I need go. And that's exactly what I did.

Sheryl "Mac" McCollum

Chapter 1

THE WOMAN IN THE BERMUDA SHORTS

ON THAT AFTERNOON, FROM THE corner of my eye, I saw the woman walk into the restaurant. Wearing Bermuda shorts, a dark blue tank top, and a simple straw hat, the middle-aged woman didn't look like she was there for the fundraiser. This was our most formal Wine & Crime to date. The restaurant was quaint and charming. The exposed brick, dark wood paneling, and heavy drapes added to the ambiance. Fine china sat on crisp white tablecloths covering the tables. The audience was dressed in their Sunday finest as if they'd just come from church. I suspected many of them had.

I had just taken the stage at Seasons Bistro in McDonough, Georgia, to introduce the speakers. The audience hung on my every word. It was October 2017, and we'd gone all out for the event. The Wine & Crime was sold out. Chef Sam had generously opened the restaurant for us on a Sunday, a day he's usually closed. He'd even designed a special cold case–themed menu featuring chicken with "capers."

After introducing the speakers, I eagerly waited offstage for my turn to present the case. The subject of this event was Drew Peterson, a police sergeant, suspected of murdering his fourth wife, Stacy Peterson. He'd already been convicted of killing his third wife, Kathleen Savio, who went missing in 2007. Stacy's body has never been found. My surprise guest that evening was Peterson's brother, who provided a unique insight into Drew's life.

Once I took the stage and began my presentation, the group was engaged and focused. I laid out the case against Peterson in minute detail. At that point, I broke through the fourth wall and asked the crowd for their help. As at other Wine & Crime events, I told them, "This ain't TV. It's time for you to go to work and help solve this case."

Wine & Crime is the most popular fundraising event for the Cold Case Investigative Research Institute (CCIRI). I founded the institute in 2004 as a collaboration between universities and colleges to bring together researchers, practitioners, students, and the criminal justice community to investigate unsolved murders.

When people ask what a Wine & Crime event is, I tell them, "I bring the murder box, you bring the wine, and together we try to develop an action plan for law enforcement on a cold case."

I'll load up the murder box—traditionally a banker's box filled with the case file. Notebooks, photographs, maps, composites, tapes, DVDs, witness statements, and other documents—everything pertaining to that cold case is in its own murder box. Together with cold case experts such as detectives, criminal profilers, victim advocates, prosecutors, and crime scene investigators like me, we present a cold case to the public.

At Wine & Crime, we present cold cases in "war room" style, allowing the attendees the opportunity to help us solve—or try to solve—each case. Guests get to play detective and use their fresh eyes to come up with insights that we professionals might have overlooked. The expert speakers give the attendees their professional perspectives on the investigative process. It's a win-win.

I simply believe if I have the ability or knowledge that might help solve a case, I should solve it and get a killer off the street. This is particularly true with cold cases, which are often the most difficult homicides to solve. The trail has gone cold. People die, evidence gets lost, memories fade, and new cases come along that need attention and resources.

That's where the CCIRI comes in and when I get to work, putting time and resources into cases we believe we can help solve. I can't imagine truly knowing I could solve a case and keeping that to myself—that is dadgum near criminal to me!

Not only are cold cases the hardest to solve, but they can also be expensive. *Very expensive.* Plus, the money we raise from events like Wine & Crime helps fund investigations into other cold cases. We never charge to investigate a cold case. *Ever!* Anyone we help receives the institute's services free. And the experts who work with us give their time, talent, and resources free of charge as well. They're never paid. Not one single dime. Why? Because they believe it's the right thing to do.

Not only are the events financially vital to the organization, but they also work! The public helps solve crimes all the time. A schoolteacher broke the Zodiac code. Abraham Shakespeare's murderer's arrest was aided by the online group Websleuths. A truck driver helped catch the DC sniper. Perhaps the best-known example is the television series *America's Most Wanted* hosted by John Walsh. The entire premise of the show is for the public to help spot and locate wanted fugitives. It's a massive success, and according to the National Center for Missing & Exploited Children, the program has been responsible for the capture of nearly 1,200 criminals. The more eyes, ears, and hands you have in a case, the better. Consider all the manpower a hundred volunteers with their different backgrounds and vocations can bring to a case.

Despite the subject matter, these events are engaging and exciting for everyone—but we never lose sight of the victim. The victim's family is always at the heart of our events and often in attendance. We're working for them, and without their insight and input, investigations can sometimes miss basic understanding and knowledge about the victim.

The woman in the Bermuda shorts stood out. She wasn't there for the meal or to discuss crimes over a few glasses of wine. Although she looked like she'd just walked in from the beach, she had a deadly serious expression on her face. She was carrying an 8 x 10 picture frame. It was clear the frame, and whatever was in it, meant something to her.

We always post a photograph of the victim on our timeline of the case back at the office. We make sure we see their faces, remember their last actions and their final place of rest. We quote them, think of them, and eventually start to think like them. I know we’re on the right track when the victim’s voice and thoughts become a natural part of how we think about the case. Then, when I work a crime scene, the case starts to roll out in my mind like a movie. I don’t see snapshots; I see the scene unfolding as it happened in real life.

The woman, her eyes bearing more pain than anyone could imagine. I’d seen the look before—too many times, to be exact—and I knew immediately why this woman in the Bermuda shorts and straw hat was there.

Staying in the back, she waited patiently until I finished my presentation. She then walked straight to me and turned the frame around. It held the photograph of a young woman. Her pretty face and wide smile was framed by neatly styled dark hair. The formal portrait showed a happy young woman with her whole life ahead of her. I could see her face in the woman standing in front of me.

The woman’s eyes betrayed the otherwise determined look about her. “This is my daughter Melissa.” She spoke in a soft, rural Georgia accent that was instantly familiar. Her pleading eyes teared up as she continued. “She was beheaded in Atlanta. Will you help me?”

Chapter 2

NORMA

I AM A CRIME SCENE investigator. It's not only a profession but also my life's purpose. The badge is the first thing I put on my uniform and the last thing I take off. It represents the oath I took and the duty I accepted willingly. At the beginning, middle, or end of any day my goal is to find the answers to unsolved crimes.

In this profession, we don't get to decide who we help and who we don't. When 9-1-1 rings, we go. Plain and simple. When someone needs us, we don't ask their religion, political affiliation, education level, race, sexual orientation—we go. We just *go*!

On a rare occasion someone will ask me, "How could you help *that* person?"

My answer is always the same. "How could we *not*?"

Society's stereotypes don't mean a thing when it comes to helping a victim or their family. It's never all right to allow a robber, rapist, or killer to walk around free.

I looked at the woman in front of me, in the straw hat and Bermuda shorts, holding a photo of her lovely daughter. I didn't know how far she had traveled to seek our help. I didn't know her backstory or her political views, or even if she graduated high school. What I did know was her daughter was beheaded in Atlanta. And no one deserves that. And this mother deserved our help. She would no longer suffer alone.

"Yes," I said. "We'll help you."

As we spoke, the guests had started talking to one another, eager to start working on their theories about whodunit in the case we'd presented. This wasn't the time or place to hold a serious discussion with a grieving mother. "Can you meet me later this week?" I asked.

We agreed to meet the following Wednesday at my office at Bauder College. I'd taught criminal justice at the college for eight years, and it was also where I started the Cold Case Investigative Research Institute.

My office is in the historic Northyards Rail Yard. It's an old, stunningly beautiful railroad roundhouse, the half-moon shape framed by red brick and iron. The first time I saw it I was struck by its historic beauty. It also provided the perfect open space to display the timelines, maps, photographs, and documents we use when investigating a cold case. It helps to lay everything out where we can all see it.

Hidden between the roundhouse and the loading area—where there are now classrooms—are abandoned railroad tracks almost entirely covered by grass and weeds. I always thought they were symbolic of what we were trying to do in that building: uncover the hidden tracks that eventually lead us to solve a case.

As I waited for the woman I knew only as "Melissa's mom" to arrive, I wracked my mind to remember ever hearing anything about an unsolved beheading of a young Caucasian woman in Atlanta. It's the kind of case you'd expect to have been all over the news—unusual, horrific, strange, and brutal. Anyone who has ever worked on a case like that never forgets it. You tend to tell the story over and over again, passing along details like a family heirloom.

But I had nothing. I'd never heard anything remotely familiar about such a case. At that point, it was still a complete blank. I was going into this without any prior knowledge.

That morning, I busied myself going over case files of what we were working on. I prepared timelines and drafted letters to various law enforcement agencies outlining investigative action plans. I also reached out to families that needed to be updated on our progress.

As I made notes, one of the CCIRI students walked into my office. "Hey, Mac. Someone is here to see you."

I looked up from my work as Melissa's mom and another younger woman came in. Both were dressed as plainly as the mother had been the previous Sunday. Melissa's mom held two large binders stuffed with documents. I welcomed them into the war room and invited them to sit.

"This is my daughter Tina," she said.

I introduced myself to Tina, telling her, like others, to call me "Mac." I then turned to Melissa's mom. "And what is your name?"

"Norma. Norma Patton."

They sat down and I pushed my files to the side. Norma placed both of her binders on the table and put a hand on top of each as if she were praying over the contents. Maybe she was. She then looked up at me with a sullen expression. I knew that expression from years of working with people who felt wronged by the system.

She took a slow, deep breath; then in a quiet, serious tone she said, "I know you said you would help, but before you do, there's something I've got to tell you."

My mind whirled with possibilities and landed on the one I heard most often. Perhaps she, like many others, didn't understand there was no cost for our services. I figured she was nervous about telling me she couldn't pay. "Okay," I said softly.

Norma steadied her hands on the binders. She looked me dead in the eyes and without flinching said, "My husband's in prison for murder, and I helped him."

Even in my line of work, that's a statement I don't hear every day. I didn't say anything at first as I contemplated my reaction. I often use humor to connect with people and figured humor might be the best way to connect with Norma. "Well then, remind me never to make you mad!"

She laughed and I laughed along with her. Her eyes cleared, and I could see her physically relax.

I asked about her husband's murder conviction and soon learned it wasn't just one. Her husband had committed five murders back in the

'70s. The more Norma talked, the more details spilled out. "Four of the five victims had been thrown in a river," she said. "I helped him dispose of two of the bodies."

At that moment, something clicked. Memories surfaced of news reports and cases I'd heard about. "Wait a minute. Is your husband the Flint River Killer?"

She nodded. "Yes."

I was familiar with the Flint River Killer, and I knew all about the Flint River. As a child, I'd played on its muddy banks. In recent years it'd become polluted as, sadly, it'd become a dumping ground. For toxins, and bodies.

Like victims of the Flint River Killer.

A couple things came to mind as I considered the way this conversation started. First, I thought, okay—this might be the most honest person I've talked to in a while. I mean, who admits to helping dispose of bodies? And second, should the sins of the father—or mother—influence how Melissa's case was handled?

Absolutely not. In my business, a victim is a victim. If a sex worker is raped, do I not have an obligation to put as much effort into her case as any other? Do I blow it off because she knew the risk? Of course not. I took an oath to help and so, I do. It's my duty.

Norma's husband was a convicted murderer, and Norma had been an accessory to his crimes. But at the end of the day, they were the parents of a murdered child. No matter what her parents had done, Melissa didn't deserve to die. Norma was the mother of a child who'd been murdered in a horrific way. And the Flint River Killer had lost a daughter to the same crime he'd committed himself.

At that moment, sitting there looking at Norma, with her hands still guarding the overflowing binders, I knew this case was different. It was unlike any other I'd ever heard of. Heck, it was unlike any case *anyone* had ever heard of.

And it was only the beginning.

Chapter 3

WHERE I COME FROM

THE FLINT RIVER, OR AS we Southerners call it—the Flint—begins right where I grew up in East Point, Georgia, a small town just south of Atlanta. As kids, the river was our secret place, a place we thought we'd discovered. I played and played there for hours and hours, pretending to be on a big adventure in some faraway place.

The river was a kid's magical hideout. We jumped in it, waded in it, and swam in it. We went frog gigging and built tiny dams to trap minnows. At the river, anything was possible, and we dreamed big. I remember thinking if I walked this whole river, I'd end up at the ocean. Maybe I'd become a pirate or an explorer and find gold and hidden treasures. But most of all, the river was a sanctuary. A sacred place for the fleeting days of childhood before the world showed us how cruel it could be.

To understand the river, you have to understand where it begins—Atlanta. Sitting at the foot of the Appalachian Mountains, Atlanta is a vibrant, diverse, and welcoming city known for its famous Peachtree Street, Peachtree Road, Peachtree Avenue, Peachtree Circle, and Piedmont Park, an urban forest on the outskirts of the city. Known as the City of Trees, Atlanta has the most trees of any urban center in the United States.

Atlanta has always provided both big-city opportunities and small-town Southern charm. People still speak to strangers on the street and will stop to help a sightseer find local landmarks or a good place to eat. In the spring when the white and pink dogwood trees are blooming, the blaze-red azaleas are in full bloom, and the yellow and orange tulips are aboveground and on glorious display, Atlanta's beauty outshines any other place in the country. My sister Sheila calls these "Chamber of Commerce Days." Driving around our city on these days, with the sun reflecting off the skyscrapers like diamonds, it's hard to imagine anything bad happening there.

There's also some pretty famous folks who hail from the city: people like Julia Roberts, Evander Holyfield, Spike Lee, 2 Chainz, Ryan Seacrest, Gladys Knight, Jeff Foxworthy, and Dr. Martin Luther King Jr. Today, Atlanta is sometimes called the Hollywood of the South due to the number of films made here. It's also home to such big corporations as Coca-Cola, Delta Air Lines, Home Depot, Chick-fil-A, and Porsche's North American headquarters.

The German luxury sports car is nice and all, but my dad, Victor Powell, worked for the insurance division of General Motors, making him a lifelong Chevy man. My mother was a genius. Seriously! She graduated from Mercer College at the age of twenty with a degree in economics and became an exceptional schoolteacher.

One of my mother's many talents was the art of storytelling. My momma could spin a yarn to keep the most fidgety child enthralled! I actually have her to thank for my interest in crime. I was all of four years old when she told me fantastic stories about Bonnie Parker and Clyde Barrow. Yes, *the* Bonnie and Clyde. Their story captivated me, and I've been fascinated by crime ever since. Some kids went to Disney World or Six Flags Over Georgia for summer break and happily reported on their adventures to their second-grade classmates. My parents took me to see Bonnie and Clyde's "Death Car." The owner of the car even let me sit in it. I remember sitting in that car, looking at all those bullet holes, and even at the tender age of eight knowing there was no way they could have escaped being shot. There was nowhere for them to have ducked or hid.

As I grew up, I begged Momma to tell me more crime stories. I longed to learn about different criminals and their crimes. She indulged my fascination with stories about Al Capone, Baby Face Nelson, and John Dillinger. I read everything I could find about Dillinger and the "lady in red."

Before I turned thirteen, my mother had taken me to see Alcatraz in San Francisco Bay, FBI Headquarters in Washington, DC, and Mafia landmarks all over the country. Despite my fascination, I learned early on from my own family that criminals weren't just names in a book or faces on WANTED posters. They were more than characters on TV. They were real people.

Momma told me story after story about her daddy's brother. Uncle Clark was a thief, a con artist, and a swindler. My momma was crazy about him! For a little girl raised in a Southern Baptist home, whose father was a preacher and mother was a Sunday school teacher, a visit from Uncle Clark was like having a carnival come to town. He was tall, handsome, a larger-than-life character before reality TV was a thing. He'd come bursting in often in the middle of the night, with some wild story of where he'd been and why he was hiding out. He'd hold her spellbound as he told stories of great adventures in exotic places, filling her mind with excitement.

Uncle Clark would often bring Momma small gifts—like the time he brought her a pair of diamond earrings when she was only six years old. Later, of course, my mother understood some poor widow or unsuspecting businessman probably got swindled out of these gifts.

Momma didn't love Uncle Clark because he was a criminal; she loved him in spite of it. To me, that made perfect sense. Family loyalty runs as deep in us as the roots of a Georgia pine. We ain't perfect, but we're family. And family always comes first. Always.

When it comes to my family, I have a saying: "Always in all ways." I'll be there whenever and wherever they need me. That thought is always on my mind each time I meet family members involved in a criminal case. I ask myself what I would do if it were my family member in this situation. And then I do it.

Loyalty is a major part of my upbringing. It's central to my life and career. I'm fiercely loyal and tend to seek out loyalty in others. I think that's why I responded to Norma like I did. Sure, she told me her husband was a murderer, and she admitted she had helped him, but I still sensed the profound loss and deep commitment to her family. I understood that kind of loyalty. That kind of commitment.

It's the same commitment and loyalty I have in my professional life as well. I met Nancy Grace when I was assigned to the major case division of the Crime Commission and she was an assistant district attorney for Fulton County. We were both in our twenties back then and formed a lifelong friendship. Nancy has gone on to do amazing things in the world of television. She was the first female to host a true-crime show. She could have had any crime analyst, CSI, or criminologist in the country to appear on her show, but she asked me.

I didn't take that honor lightly. Because I respect her so much, I wanted to give her my all and do the best job possible. That meant getting advanced degrees in criminal justice, obtaining police standards certificates, gaining a wide variety of law enforcement experience, and sharing my expertise whenever asked through the CCIRI.

All of that still enriches my career and enables me to support those in need, but it's not who *I am*. Through years of education and experience, I've learned a lot about crime and criminals. I also learned a lot about myself. Working different crime scenes, you learn who you really are. Reality doesn't stop at the yellow tape roping off a scene. As you step over that threshold, you bring with it all your faith, fears, troubles, training, triumphs, failures, and successes. And none of that matters more than the fact that I am, first and foremost, a mother.

I have two children—son, Huck, and daughter, Caroline. They are two and a half years apart. After becoming a mother, you begin to see the world differently. I bring that perspective to work every day, and I'll tell you straight up, before my kids were born, I was a different criminal justice expert. Because of Huck and Caroline, my work is more personal now. Because of them, I am braver and more committed and unyielding in my fight for justice. I also cry a lot easier—mostly sentimental and happy tears—but still tears, nonetheless.

As a parent, I knew that to help Norma find who had killed and beheaded her daughter sixteen years ago, I had to know more about her husband and Melissa's father, Carl Patton. And not just Carl's crimes, but about Carl, a killer himself.

Chapter 4

CARL: THE KILLER

IT WASN'T UNUSUAL FOR ME to call on a killer for help with a case. In my business, if you want to understand why someone would kill, you ask someone who's been there, done that. You ask another killer.

If I was going to find Melissa's killer, what better resource did I have than someone who not only knew Melissa but had also killed? The best person to help me solve her murder was a murderer himself—her father, Carl Patton.

As an investigator, I'm extraordinarily analytical. I look at the big picture, then break it down bit by bit. I needed to know Carl Patton. More importantly, I needed to know about his crimes. I was aware of the Flint River killings but had never studied them. I'd never taken a deep dive. I remember thinking, *Honey, put your scuba gear on, 'cause we're going diving.*

I learned through Norma that her husband was a man who called his own shots. He made his own rules, and he ran with dangerous friends. Carl Patton was a dangerous man, defiantly violent, someone who stood his ground—every inch of it—and never backed down. Carl took care of his family and did what he thought was right at the time to protect them, no matter the cost. He saw his actions as loyalty, and if you got in his way, well, he could be cruel, violent, unfeeling, and unforgiving.

And he could kill.

Carl Millard Patton Jr. killed for the first time in 1973 when he was just twenty-four years old. At that time, he and Norma had been married five years; their daughter, Tina Mae, was three years old when Carl pointed a gun at a man and pulled the trigger.

The victim was Richard Jackson, the husband of acquaintance Marie Jackson. Marie claimed her husband was abusive and offered Carl $2,500 of a life insurance policy to kill him. Carl accepted the offer and enlisted lifelong friend Joe Cleveland to help him.

On March 9, 1973, with Cleveland following, Carl lured Richard Jackson to his car and drove him to a wooded area near Ellenwood, Georgia. Once parked, Carl pulled out a .22-caliber pistol. Jackson realized what was about to happen and bolted from the vehicle. Carl and Cleveland chased him down, then shot and killed him, shooting him a total of eight times. Norma didn't know about Jackson's murder at that time.

By 1977, Carl and Norma had moved to Ellenwood. Melissa was born that September, making the Pattons a family of four. However, Carl was apparently untroubled by killing Jackson four years earlier, or at least untroubled enough to agree to kill for money once again.

Marie Jackson, who then went by Marie Wyatt, approached Carl again. This time, the target was Carl's own uncle and Marie's former common-law husband, Fred Wyatt, and his new girlfriend, Betty Jo Ephlin. Marie was upset that Fred had left her for Betty Jo. She offered to split a $30,000 insurance policy on Wyatt if he'd kill them both. Carl pulled in Joe Cleveland again to help him.

Carl shot Ephlin and Wyatt, drugging Wyatt first. He shot Wyatt in the ear. Norma witnessed the murders.

Carl and Cleveland chained a concrete block to Betty Jo, then dumped her lifeless body in the Flint River. They placed Wyatt's body in a car and left it on some railroad tracks, staging what they hoped would look like an accident when hit by the train.

With an indescribable coldness, Carl and Norma even took some of Betty Jo's belongings, clothes, jewelry, and furniture to their own home. Betty Joe's daughter, Linda, told police while serving a search warrant that

Norma was wearing a vest that was owned by her mother. Melissa was just a little over two months old.

A short time later, Carl grew paranoid that his buddy Joe Cleveland had talked. Specifically, to his girlfriend, Liddie Evans. Carl knew Cleveland was a talker, a guy who liked to run his mouth. He often bragged about his criminal escapades and ties with the infamous Dixie Mafia. In Carl's eyes, this made Cleveland not only a bad business partner but a liability. If anyone talked, Carl could be sent to prison, leaving Norma to raise their girls on her own. Carl wouldn't put that kind of burden on his wife. He wouldn't let his daughters grow up with their daddy in prison, unable to provide for them and protect them.

He decided he'd eliminate the problem. Although Norma tried to talk him out of it, Carl had made up his mind: He had to kill Joe Cleveland and Liddie Evans.

Carl lured Cleveland and Evans to his home. According to Norma, the two men began playfully tossing a pistol back and forth until Carl decided the time was right. Playtime was over. He shot Evans twice and Cleveland once, killing both. Norma helped him drag the bodies outside and into a camper van. There, they wrapped them in sleeping bags. Carl, once again, attached concrete blocks to his latest victims. Liddie Evan's body was tossed into the Flint River while Joe Cleveland was dumped into the nearby Ocmulgee River. Norma helped him.

Norma would later admit in court that while Carl burned several pieces of their bloodstained furniture in the backyard, she cleaned up, wiping away most of the incriminating evidence. At least she thought she did.

In late 1977, Carl and Norma were questioned about Cleveland's and Evans's murders when their bodies were found just days after being dumped. Once bloodstains were found in the trunk of his car, Carl became a prime suspect. He was even arrested but wasn't charged, and he was released shortly after on lack of evidence. This was years before DNA evidence could definitively prove the source of the blood as Cleveland's or Evans's. But deep in their guts, the investigators involved knew Carl was their man.

Although only two of Carl Patton's five victims were actually found in the Flint River, local media dubbed the unknown perpetrator "the Flint River Killer." And thus was born a serial killer.

Chapter 5

MELISSA

FOR THE NEXT TWENTY-ONE YEARS, the Pattons lived a relatively quiet life. Aside from a 1983 arrest for theft and a short jail sentence, Carl remained out of trouble and out of prison. He and Norma went about their daily lives of work and raising Tina Mae and Melissa.

Carl worked as a carpenter, mainly as a roofer, and at one time owned his own business. Norma kept the books.

Growing up, Melissa had been a typical young girl, taking baton lessons and following her older sister around. Tina remembers Melissa as very loving. "If she loved you, you knew it, and she just had a lot of dreams when she was in school."

I'm told by her mother that Melissa made good grades in school and was even in the high school branch of the ROTC. She had friends and appeared to have a bright future ahead of her. She was growing into a beautiful, bright young lady.

All that changed when Melissa was in high school and met Christopher Wolfenbarger. *She* changed, and not for the better. She started sneaking out at night to meet Christopher. According to Norma, he even talked Melissa into stealing Carl's car, not once, but twice! Neither her parents nor her sister cared for Christopher very much from the start. Norma said she saw "meanness in his eyes."

Christopher pressured Melissa to run away with him to California, and in 1994 they did run away, but not to California. They ended up in

Oklahoma. They were caught after Christopher, who'd been driving 120 miles an hour at night, the wrong way on the interstate, hit a bull after exiting the freeway.

But that didn't stop the two misguided lovebirds from seeing each other. Both were in and out of trouble, and both were arrested several times. Melissa became pregnant with a daughter, Christina, and she and Christopher soon married. But Carl and Norma were only allowed to see their granddaughter when Christopher was at work. By 1998 Melissa had given birth to another baby, a boy they named Joey. By this time they had moved to Atlanta, and Melissa worked when she could, often waitressing at a Waffle House.

The marriage was troubled from the start. Melissa and Christopher were young, poor, and lacked the education and skills to get good jobs. Life wasn't easy for them, and as sometimes happens in similar situations, they took it out on one another.

Melissa often had bruises on her arms and neck. One day she showed up at the Waffle House and told Tina that Christopher had beaten her and dragged her down the street.

The relationship was toxic and volatile. So much so, local police became accustomed to being called to their house. Melissa sometimes called them to report that Christopher was beating on her, and Christopher sometimes called and claimed Melissa had struck him, something Melissa's family didn't then and still doesn't believe she ever did. After one beating at the hands of her husband, Melissa even left Christopher for a while. He was charged with domestic violence, but when they went before the judge, Christopher managed to talk Melissa out of pressing charges.

I'd seen that scene play out over and over again, and it never ended happily ever after. Same play, different actors.

November 9, 1998, was the last time Melissa Wolfenbarger's momma would ever see her alive. Thanksgiving would be the last time she'd ever talk to her baby. She told her mother that she was with Christopher.

Norma remembers they'd made tentative plans for Christmas. It was during that conversation when Melissa asked her momma for a special

Christmas present. It wasn't anything Norma could go out and buy at any store, like a pretty sweater or a necklace. It was much more meaningful than those things could ever be.

All she wanted was a copy of a photograph of her beloved PawPaw, Carl's daddy. Norma promised her she'd find one for her. A good one, too, one that she could cherish forever and would be all hers. As most mothers do, Norma ended the phone call by saying, "I love you, and you know where I am if you need me."

Maybe it was maternal instinct, but at that time, Norma had no other way of knowing just how true those words were or how much Melissa would truly need her.

Christmas came and went, and the 8 x 10 photograph of Melissa's granddaddy sat unopened under the decorated tree. Norma had kept her promise and excitedly wrapped the photo. She couldn't wait to see the expression on Melissa's face when she opened it.

Over the years, Carl and Norma had grown used to not hearing from Melissa that often. That year, they reckoned that maybe she was just feeling overwhelmed, what with two little ones and the rush of the holidays. Or maybe Christopher wouldn't allow her to visit them and she didn't want to make him mad. Maybe that's why she hadn't come home for Christmas. At least that's what they told one another.

But day after day went by and while life settled into the new year, Norma couldn't shake the feeling something wasn't right. Carl and Tina weren't too concerned, saying it wasn't the first time they'd gone awhile without hearing from Melissa. But for Norma, the uneasy feeling persisted. She couldn't escape the ominous thought something was wrong. Dead wrong.

Norma wondered if Melissa had moved. After all, bless her heart, a lot of her life had been lived out of a suitcase. As far as she and Carl knew, Melissa was still living in Atlanta with Christopher and their children. Carl and Norma were living in Locust Grove at that time. Being about an hour south of Atlanta, depending on traffic and which route you took, the distance wasn't too far, but far enough it wasn't always easy to visit one another. Melissa didn't always have a car, and there had been times Christopher forbade his wife from seeing her parents.

Melissa had only a small circle of social contacts. She had few friends, if any, and never had that all-important best friend to visit with. She was quiet and tended to keep to herself. Truthfully, after she and Christopher married, she didn't see Carl and Norma that often. Carl and Christopher didn't get along, and there was no need to throw fuel on a simmering fire. Norma never wanted to make things more difficult for her youngest daughter.

That February, Norma anxiously waited for a call, a card, anything from Melissa. It wasn't like her to miss her momma's birthday. It wasn't like her at all. Melissa had never missed wishing Norma a happy birthday. After the usually happy occasion had come and gone with still no contact, Norma *really* started to worry. This time, Carl agreed. Melissa would never, ever, miss calling her momma on her special day.

They began looking for her everywhere they could think of. They even checked with Waffle House to see if she still worked for the company at a different location. She didn't. Carl reached out to Tina and asked if she'd heard from Melissa lately. When Tina told him no, the father and daughter headed for Atlanta, to the last known address Melissa had shared with Christopher.

What they found was a deserted house and neighbors who told them they thought they'd moved out right around Christmas or the first of the year. Just up and left without telling anyone. Carl and Norma then headed to Action Glass & Mirror, the company Christopher worked for the last time they had heard from Melissa. There, they learned Christopher had been fired in December after getting into a hit-and-run accident in one of the company trucks. No one at the company had talked to him since.

No one knew where Christopher Wolfenbarger was. Or his two little children—Carl and Norma's grandchildren—Christina and Joey.

Wracked with worry, Norma went to her local police department in Henry County. She tried to file a missing persons report, but the police told her there wasn't anything they could do. Melissa had been living in

Atlanta, and they couldn't take a report from another jurisdiction. So, Norma headed to Atlanta.

The Atlanta police explained to her that since Melissa was an adult, she could leave town whenever she wanted. Christopher, her lawful husband, hadn't reported her missing, and no acquaintances or neighbors had contacted the police to report anything suspicious about her disappearance. Their hands were tied. After all, it wasn't against the law to just drop out of sight.

On April 29, 1999, a human skull was found stuffed into a ripped plastic garbage bag on Avon Avenue in Atlanta. Authorities later concluded the skull belonged to a white male. A few days later in Twiggs County, a headless man was found in a ditch, but the skull from Atlanta didn't match the body. In June, four more trash bags were located near where the head was discovered, containing dismembered arms and legs. But no torso.

No one suspected that the skull or body parts might belong to Melissa. Why would they? They believed the skull belonged to a white male. And as far as the police were concerned, Melissa wasn't even a missing person. No one named Christopher Wolfenbarger had ever reported their wife missing. No one had ever filed a missing persons report.

Apart from Carl, Norma, and Tina, no one else was looking for Melissa.

Sure, the discarded body parts had Atlanta Police puzzled, but there had been no reported missing white males in the Metro Atlanta area at that time. With nothing else to go on, the case grew cold.

And still, no one knew where Melissa was. At least no one said they did.

As winter turned to spring and spring to summer, Norma felt a deepening panic—she couldn't find her child. Carl Patton wasn't scared of nothing but by then, even he was scared. As parents you know your children, and Norma and Carl knew that by then Melissa would have contacted them if she could. If she couldn't, it was because something bad had happened to her. Norma was sure of that in her heart. She felt like her world was spinning out of control. Not being able to find her daughter, her flesh and blood—a child she'd given birth to—made her feel like she was losing her mind. Early on in the whole ordeal, Norma couldn't bring herself to think it, let alone say it. If she said the word, she feared it'd make it real. But by the fall of 1999, Norma Patton feared her child was dead.

It would be a long, long time before that fear materialized into reality. It would be an even longer time before she and Carl would know that truth. The truth of what really happened to Melissa.

Chapter 6

THE BEGINNING OR THE END: 2003

CARL PATTON HAD GOTTEN AWAY with murder and lived a free man for twenty-five years. Up until 1998 when Melissa went missing, his world didn't change much from the days before he murdered five people. He still worked hard for Norma and the girls. Most of all, he enjoyed his family. He enjoyed spending time with them and loving on Norma.

In 2003, Carl's freedom came to an abrupt end. During the twenty-five years he'd remained free, investigators continued working the Flint River murders. Year by year, the use of DNA grew. With dogged police work, coupled with the DNA evidence, investigators were finally able to connect Carl to the killings of Joe Cleveland and Betty Jo Ephlin.

Once arrested, Carl immediately confessed. Not only did he admit what he'd done, he later said he began to feel remorse. Until Melissa went missing, he didn't understand the tragedy of his crimes. Now he understood how it felt to live like that.

He pled guilty and was sentenced to two life terms with a chance of parole after serving twenty years. Extradited to DeKalb County, he was then charged with the Cleveland–Evans murders. Norma cooperated with the authorities and provided testimony against her husband. She, too, pled guilty, but due to her cooperation, she received only twelve months' probation and a $1,000 fine. Carl then pled guilty to the other murders as well and received two additional life terms.

Oddly enough, Carl's arrest gave him and Norma one of the answers they had feared. Their daughter Melissa was dead.

As in standard procedure, Carl's DNA was run through the system. Investigators were looking for any additional victims of the man known as the Flint River Killer. They were surprised when they got a hit. Not that they weren't anticipating more victims, but they were stunned with the results.

Carl's DNA matched that of the dismembered body parts discarded in Atlanta in 1999. Law enforcement then took DNA from Norma and compared it to Melissa's. They also compared Melissa's dental records with the skull found near the body parts.

Everything was a match. The discarded skull and body parts belonged to Melissa Wolfenbarger, Carl and Norma Patton's daughter.

Carl was quickly cleared of any involvement in her death, but the irony was obvious: Carl and Norma, whose own crimes had victimized so many others, leaving friends and family members to wonder how their loved ones had been killed and why, became victims themselves. As parents of a murdered young woman, they were now left to worry over the same questions.

A serial killer had become the victim of a murderer himself.

The more I learned about the Pattons, the more determined I became to not let their pasts deter me from helping Melissa. She had nothing to do with her parents' crimes. She had been an innocent twenty-one-year-old young wife and mother who didn't deserve to be decapitated and have her body parts strewn about like garbage.

Her children deserved better. Her family deserved better. And Melissa deserved better.

Did I feel sympathy for Carl Patton? In this case, I did. He was a grieving father. But to be very clear, Carl Patton absolutely did what he did. He admitted to his crimes and deserved to be right where he was—in prison.

There was no need to waste breath or argue whether he was guilty of the crimes he was accused of. No need to argue whether he was a serial killer. There's absolutely no argument there.

But in what world does that mean Melissa, and her children, her sister, and her parents, do not deserve justice? Was Melissa's life less valuable because of the crimes of her parents? Just because of the sins of her father and mother, does that mean a killer gets to go free?

No. Jim Leffman, a former United States Secret Service agent, said it best: "Never look down at anyone, unless extending a hand to pick them back up."

That's all I was doing. I thought Melissa deserved that.

I had known nothing about Norma's past prior to meeting with her. I knew nothing about Carl Patton. And although I had heard of the Flint River murders, I knew next to nothing about them.

In my business, in the real world at the police department, we don't get to pick and choose who we help and who we don't. If there is a victim of crime, we help that person, period. We help.

Chapter 7

THE INVESTIGATION BEGINS: THE BACKGROUND

AFTER MEETING NORMA THAT FIRST time, then getting to know her and agreeing to look for Melissa's killer, I often thought of the photograph she had brought with her to the Wine & Crime. The afternoon she asked for my help.

There are two walls in my office dedicated to the cold cases I've worked. One wall contains items from cases that at that time are still unsolved, cases we're still actively working.

The other wall is dedicated to cases we *have* solved, cases that are now closed and whose families now have an answer. And each time we close a case, I contact my friend, Kelly Lawson, the forensic artist for the Georgia Bureau of Investigation.

Kelly is gifted and shares her talent for composite drawings graciously. Her drawings of suspects are shared with police from all over the state to help them in their jobs. She sits with witnesses and transcribes their descriptions into a drawing of a suspect's face. To witness Kelly at work, to watch her listen to a victim who was brutally attacked describe their assailant, and then see the pencil start moving as she begins to draw, and then you see the strokes and angles take shape and a face slowly appears, well, you know then you're watching a talent from beyond. Kelly is one of the experts in the CCIRI as well as an expert I have used at my department. With the CCIRI she has done a retro composite for the Golden

State Killer, a suspect age progression of the kidnapper in the Vi Ripken case, and age progression of the Nacole Smith killer, and the closed case portrait of Honey Malone.

Many people can draw, paint, or sculpt incredible works of beauty. What Kelly does transcends artistic boundaries. I would say God works through her.

Kelly also uses her gift in the most incredible way for me with my cold cases. When we close a case, she gives me a drawing of the victim. The drawings go on the wall of solved cases. They remind me daily that justice prevailed, and families have answers.

The drawings are all important to me. When people visit my office and ask me about one or more of the faces that stare back at them, I tell their story. It's my private way of keeping their memories alive.

Someday I wanted to look up and see a drawing of Melissa looking back at me from that wall, and I wanted to tell her story.

In April 1999, the skull was found. It was mistakenly categorized as that of a Caucasian male. Two months later, in June, four trash bags were found near where the skull had been found. Each bag contained an arm or a leg, but no torso. At that time, the Atlanta Police Department didn't have any reports of a missing Caucasian male.

Precious time was lost from April to June by not having all of the bags located at the same time as the skull to piece together all the evidence. Was the victim transient or was he from out of state? Was this a mob hit? Was this person connected to a drug cartel? Where was the rest of his body? Why here?

So many questions with so few answers. What about the suspects? Well, there weren't any. Without knowing who the victim was, law enforcement certainly didn't have any idea who would want to harm the man. The police had nothing more to go on than what they'd found in the bags.

Remember, Norma went to the local police department in Henry County to report Melissa missing. Officers there gently explained they couldn't take a missing persons report for another jurisdiction, and since Melissa lived in Atlanta, that's where Norma would need to file a report.

So, her momma went to Atlanta and tried to make a report, and Atlanta efficiently explained to her that Melissa was a married woman. She could leave town if she wanted to. They had no evidence that anything had happened to her. Her husband hadn't reported her missing. Friends, neighbors—nobody had told them anything nefarious had occurred.

Norma couldn't get law enforcement to take a report, couldn't get them to start a search, and couldn't get them to open an investigation into her daughter's whereabouts. Besides, the only unidentified remains found recently belonged to a Caucasian male.

One of the first steps in an investigation like this is to develop what's called the victimology. What factors contributed to Melissa's murder? Was it her lifestyle? Her environment? To get the answers you need, you go to the people who knew the victim best. I asked Melissa's momma Norma, her sister Tina Mae, and last but not least, her daddy, Carl Patton, to help us put it together. Carl would serve a dual purpose: as Melissa's father, and as someone who had killed five people in cold blood.

Norma: "Melissa was…she was quiet. She loved animals. It didn't matter whether it was a dog or a cat or a rabbit or whatever. I had to keep a rabbit for my sister for a little while, and Melissa went with me to pick the rabbit up. She basically took care of the rabbit. I was supposed to be the one taking care of it, but she took care of the rabbit. But that's just—she loved animals. It didn't matter what it was, she just—she loved them. She loved everybody."

When I spoke with Tina, I told her I knew she and Melissa had been close. I have four sisters myself. I knew what that bond was like. I asked Tina to tell me about her sister.

Tina: "She was quiet, like Mom said, but, you know, she loved animals. And if she loved you, then you definitely knew she loved you. But she kind of, you know she was shy. She kept to herself. The only way she met new people was through people she already knew."

I wanted to know from Norma when she'd first felt something in her gut, when she knew something was wrong.

Norma: "When she didn't come at Christmas or call because she had asked me for something in particular, and she said that was all…the only thing she wanted, and it wasn't something that I could go to the store and buy. It was something I had to…had to find. And what it was, was a picture of her with her PawPaw—her daddy's father. And that's all she wanted was that picture. So, I found a picture of him and her together and she was only five years old, maybe six at the most. And I took it and had it blown up into an 8 x 10 and had it wrapped up and under the Christmas tree and she didn't call. She didn't…didn't come get it, you know, and that was just…that wasn't like her."

At that point, I asked Tina to verify when she and her daddy, Carl, became worried. Tina and her daddy weren't as concerned about Melissa's whereabouts as her momma. Melissa had been known to not show up before for different reasons. Cell phones were still a thing of the future. She didn't always have a car. She didn't always have a way to get to them or contact them.

Tina: "I didn't get concerned until I was at work one morning at a Waffle House in East Point, and here comes my dad walking in the door talking about, 'Where's your sister?' I said, 'I don't know. Why?' She hasn't worked with me in a while now, you know, a few months at least—at least six months. And he said, 'Because we can't find her; she didn't show up for Christmas.' And I was like, what? She didn't show up for Christmas? 'And she didn't call your mom and tell her a happy birthday either.' And I was like, wait a minute. Something's wrong. If she doesn't call Mom and tell her happy birthday, something's really wrong."

What I knew so far was Melissa's life wasn't always that easy. She had some issues in her marriage. They were young and poor. They didn't have the education or skills for a good job. They had two small babies. They both had criminal records. Life was hard for them. She had some issues with the police. She had been to jail a couple of times for small-time stuff like shoplifting or fighting. I asked Norma and Tina if they had checked jails and hospitals, and they said they did and she wasn't anywhere. I asked where else they had checked.

Norma: "Where didn't we check? I even called the main Waffle House and talked to somebody in personnel to find out if she was working at another location somewhere, and they did not have her as an employee anywhere, which surprised me that they bothered to check. But once I got into telling her why I was…was asking the question and, you know, she looked, according to their records and couldn't find Melissa as an employee. So, that really, really shook me up. Me and Carl went to Atlanta on Brookline Street where they were living after Carl talked to Tina. The house was completely deserted. We talked to some of the neighbors, and they said that he moved out of the house right around Christmas, or the first of the year he up and left. And they told us where he was working at. We went over there and talked to the owner of the company, and they said they had fired him because he had gotten in a hit-and-run in one of their trucks and he wasn't where he was supposed to be. So, they fired him in December. At that point, we just didn't know."

While Carl was in prison, I asked him when he had started to get worried. He responded in a letter, "I wasn't that worried about Melissa in the first few days because she didn't have a phone and couldn't call us. I became extremely worried after Mother's Day. I knew then it was bad. There's no way Melissa wouldn't call or come by on Mother's Day."

Carl also shared a key piece of information: Christopher was afraid of him. Carl knew if something had happened to Melissa that Christopher would be too scared to come tell him.

This type of intel was vitally important to the investigation. Understanding that Carl disliked, distrusted, and once physically attacked Christopher was crucial. Carl told me that Christopher fled after the murder. Carl said Christopher lived under an assumed name. Carl said sure made him wonder. Though Christopher could be expecting his wife to return home one day.

At this point, it'd been about a year since anyone had heard from Melissa. As a mother myself, I'm gonna tell you straight up: Melissa might have left her house, she might have left her husband, but she would not have left her two children!

In 1998, the year Melissa went missing, her little girl was three and the little boy was two. They're grown adults now.

Norma made one thing clear: "Her kids were her life."

Tina echoed her mother, adding how much Melissa wanted the kids in her life: "She left her husband once but went back because of the kids."

Norma verified there was often turmoil in the marriage: "They had some domestic violence in their marriage. I mean, it's documented in police reports. And sometimes she would call the police on him, and sometimes he'd call the police on her, and it was volatile." According to Calhoun police report Christopher was arrested thirteen times between 1994 and 2000 for crimes like thefts, aggravated assault, battery, and marijuana possession.

Tina added: "It was more volatile on his end, not on hers, because she wasn't a violent person. She wouldn't fight you. And that's important to know."

With everything they'd told me so far, the information was beginning to paint a picture of who Melissa was. She was a young mother of two, in a volatile marriage to her first love, poor, uneducated, minor criminal record, sporadic employment, and deeply devoted to her family.

Norma shared that she remembered the moment the panic set in. Her world was spinning out of control—not being able to find her child was causing her to feel like she was losing her mind. But Carl was her rock, her constant, her protector. If anyone could find Melissa and make this nightmare end, it was Carl.

The moment she realized Carl, the man who feared nothing, was scared, Norma panicked. Soon after, her world was knocked off its axis.

Chapter 8

CARL AND NORMA'S ARREST: THE CONNECTION

CARL PATTON WAS ARRESTED IN 2003 for the murders of Fred Wyatt, Betty Jo Ephlin, Joe Cleveland, and Liddie Evans. He confessed to the four murders and then told detectives there was a fifth victim. Carl added Richard Jackson to the list of his victims. Norma was arrested, too, but in a twist. Norma was arrested after she agreed to and did testify against Carl for immunity from prosecution.

However, it wasn't like Norma had thrown Carl under the proverbial bus. The two had already discussed it and agreed to the plan. Norma and Carl agreed that they would go to court and tell the truth, and both admit to what happened and what they'd done. Carl committed the murders. Norma helped him dispose of the bodies.

Major Bruce Jordan with the Fayette County Sheriff's Office was the investigator who broke the case and made the arrests. When Carl and Norma were arrested, Melissa had been missing over four years.

The Pattons began to look at Major Jordan not as the man who arrested them but as someone who might be able to help them find their daughter.

Brimming with hope, Carl said, "He caught me after twenty-five years. He must be a pretty good detective."

Norma agreed and arranged to meet with Major Jordan. She said, "My daughter Melissa is missing. Will you please help find her?"

He told Norma he'd absolutely help her. He went to the prison to talk to Carl. He then talked to Norma. He gathered the information he needed to get started in the search for Melissa.

One of the first things Jordan realized was Melissa's husband, Christopher Wolfenbarger, worked at Action Glass & Mirror on Avon Avenue. And Avon Avenue was where the skull was found back in 1999. At that time, Norma and Carl knew nothing about a found skull or the dismembered body parts located just feet away from where their former son-in-law had worked.

With this new information, Jordan headed to the Atlanta Police Department. "Look," he said. "This skull was found just a few feet away from where a missing woman's husband works. Don't you think it could be her?"

They agreed and on March 13, 2003, they got the dental records for Melissa and had the medical examiner compare them with the skull. Sure enough, it was a match. On March 14, the skull was positively identified as Melissa Wolfenbarger.

Law enforcement had lost four years! Four years without a homicide investigation. Four long years where a killer not only walked free but was not a suspect. Not just free but without being hunted.

Melissa's momma had reported her missing to both Henry County and Atlanta. Henry County couldn't do anything because Melissa had lived in Atlanta. Atlanta couldn't do anything because she'd been married so her husband would have to be the one to report her as missing. The police needed to see that some overt act had happened to her. But there was no blood anywhere. There were no windows broken out of the home. No calls for emergency help. No one had heard screams or seen anything suspicious. There was nothing to lead anyone to believe a crime had been committed against Melissa Wolfenbarger.

This was maddening for her family. They knew the police were right but had no proof other than their gut feeling.

In 2003, four years after her parents feared something bad had happened, Melissa Wolfenbarger was officially declared deceased. Was her husband, Christopher, who had been her high school sweetheart, responsible? They'd had a relationship that was volatile. They fought. They argued. Police were called. Sometimes arrests were made. They had been in and out of jail. They had been on and off probation. But despite their interactions with the police, nothing either of them had ever done had reached the felony level.

Was there a long list of suspects? No. There was only one. Not the number one suspect, but *the* suspect. For me, there was only one suspect: Christopher Wolfenbarger. My entire focus was on Melissa's husband.

He was the last person to see her alive. She had no car, no money, no clothes, and no cell phone when she supposedly left on her own. He never reported her missing. He never called her family about her whereabouts. He never told the children anything bad happened to her or where she was. He never checked with police or hospitals or the morgue. He never looked for her. He worked on the same street where the skull was found. He worked within feet of where dismembered arms and legs were found. He had a past that was violent. He had a hit-and-run in a work truck. He moved out of town after she went missing. He seemed to know she wasn't coming back.

After Melissa was identified, Christopher did not pick up her remains from the funeral home, and he didn't pay for the funeral. He was not afraid a killer was on the loose and might come and hurt him or his children. And prior to her going missing, his mother had gotten Melissa to sign over custody of her children to her! How was this not a red flag for everyone? Why would Melissa do that? Was she fearful she might be going to jail? She was on probation. Perhaps out of caution she wanted to be certain if something happened the children had legal care inside the family. But why not her own mother? Or sister? Was she being controlled by Christopher? Was this a result of mental abuse to find a way to take her children from her? At best, Christopher was going to be the callous guy who didn't look for her, didn't bury her, didn't make sure the children were okay with what happened to their momma. At worst he was her killer.

Despite the knowledge they'd gained into Melissa's murder, Major Jordan and the Atlanta Police Department hit a wall. Though Norma, Tina, and Carl had heard about me through my high school friend, Donna Jones. He asked Norma to reach out to me. After meeting with Norma, my mind went to DNA on the trash bags, crime mapping, statement analysis, getting Christopher to make additional statements…I wanted to throw everything we had at this case. And so did Carl.

I remember he asked me if I thought Nancy Grace in the DA's office would talk about Melissa sometime. "I think she'd be great on her case," he'd said.

I jokingly said, "Who?"

Carl would laugh and say, "She might just go right up to Christopher and start asking him questions on camera."

Chapter 9

LOYALTY

IT'S IMPORTANT TO NOTE THAT Christopher Wolfenbarger denied any involvement in Melissa's murder. However, Sergeant Raymond Layton from the Atlanta Police Department's homicide squad told *Dateline* that Wolfenbarger had an "extensive criminal history with family violence." Witnesses also stated during the investigation that he had been abusive to Melissa.

During an interview for the same *Dateline* segment, Christopher declared, "I'm not denying I have a criminal history. We were, you know, like Bonnie and Clyde, just small-time criminals, but we didn't do anything bad." He further told *Dateline* that when Melissa never returned home, he figured she'd changed her identity and went on to live her dream without him in California.

We were anxious to see the interview with *Dateline.* We believed based on past articles that he would talk to a reporter. We knew there was a chance he would respond and then act out.

Norma started to suspect Melissa's husband as her daughter's killer early on. She said, "As my mother would say, it was the look in his eyes when I met him. You could just see the…the meanness in his eyes. I didn't like him and it just, it went downhill from there." Norma never trusted him either, even in high school. She said, "He had Melissa climbing out the bedroom window and sneaking out to go wherever he wanted to go, and I always reported her as a runaway. They run away in December of 1994 and ended up in Oklahoma. The police called me and told me that they caught him driving the wrong way on the interstate doing 120 miles an hour with no lights on. He went off the interstate and hit a bull. Anyway, they lost track of him, but they caught up with him. When they caught up with him, he laughed at them. He said, 'The only reason you caught me is because I hit that bull.' So that's his…the way he always looked at everything."

In cases of domestic violence, we often find the victim doesn't seek help or make an outcry. Tina said that Melissa "didn't talk about them. I knew about them. You know, me and her worked at the Waffle House close to the airport one time together and, at night…she came in one night with a handprint around her throat. Her eyes were red. She had been crying. And I knew what it was. I knew. It was Chris. When I asked her about it, she said, 'Don't say anything.' And I was like, 'Oh, no, no, no, no. I'm going to say something.' And I did.

"And so did my boyfriend at the time and, you know, he reached across and slapped him and said something to him, and Chris just turned his head and looked out the window like it was nothing."

But Christopher didn't retaliate when a man was involved. It's classic with abusers. They're only badass when they have a soft target. The wife, the children, the pets. The ones that can't fight back.

Both Tina and Carl had thought about avenging Melissa's murder. But they both had their reasons for not killing the killer. Ironically, it was the same reason: family.

Carl told me in a letter, "I promised Norma I wouldn't kill nobody else."

Like a lot of daughters, Tina loves her daddy. She thinks like him. Plans and plots like him. She holds her family together like her daddy. The death of her baby sister rocked her deeper than she even knew.

She said it wasn't until after they knew Melissa had been murdered that she realized just how much she loved her. That sister bond is unbreakable even in death. Tina was fearless, strong, and, just like her daddy, loyal. She wanted to confront the man she believed killed her sister, but she didn't. She wouldn't risk messing up the future case or going to jail herself. She needed to be free for her kids and grandkids, her momma and Melissa, as well as her dad.

This bears repeating: Carl Patton was loyal to a fault, and he called his own shots. He ran with dangerous friends. He was a dangerous man. He was defiantly violent and stood his ground—every inch of it. I never for a minute forgot who I was dealing with, a killer. I asked him multiple times if he was connected to the Dixie Mafia. I saw some major similarities between the two. Of course, he denied any association with the Dixie Mafia, although one of his close associates was known to brag that they were members. What Carl saw as loyalty others saw as unforgiving reactions. He would do anything to protect his interests, his home, and his family. Including kill.

Family loyalty is at its strongest when a child is involved. My sister Sharon is not a criminal. Has never been arrested or had an issue with the police. But she understands protecting children.

Once, our niece was having an issue with her biological father. My knee-jerk reaction is to dog cuss someone out and make threats. Not Sharon. She was slow and deliberate with her response. She took a step toward the father and said, "I'd kill for my child!"

She then slowly raised her arm and pointed at our niece while locking eyes with her father said, "And *that's* my child."

Melissa's murder changed Carl. For the first time in his life, he was forced to look at his own crimes from the families of the victims' perspective. It was gut-wrenching to feel what he then knew he had put others through. He had never experienced loss at the hands of another. Much less the loss of a child.

And he was helpless in prison. He had no way to search for Melissa or hunt for clues and evidence for the police. He was trapped in a cell with his own thoughts and feelings. He had become used to the brutal prison environment, but it was not being able to help find Melissa that was killing him. It was hell emotionally and mentally.

Then came the news that was not a total shock but still devastating: Melissa had been murdered. Some of her remains had been recovered. His baby daughter had not just been murdered, she had been beheaded and dismembered.

Carl could hardly function. He wasn't there for Norma and Tina. He couldn't comfort them and protect them from the killer. He often thought about *his* victims—Richard, Fred, Betty Jo, Liddie, and even his lifelong friend, Joe Cleveland. Now, Carl was forced to feel the same pain, anguish, and misery their loved ones had felt because of him. It was overwhelming. To be punished with this karma-like loss was unbearable.

With Carl in prison, Norma drove six hours round trip each week to visit with her husband. "I don't know how to put it," she said. "His arrest and finding out what happened to Melissa, it just made him realize what he had done to the families of the people that he had killed. That just…it kinda…knocked him for a loop, for lack of a better way of putting it. He just feels he let Melssia down because he didn't protect her."

Carl did all he could do from behind bars to find Melissa's killer. We corresponded for years through letters. And, through those letters, Carl said similar things to me, that he'd had no idea what he had done to the families of his victims. Not only was he wracked with remorse for what he'd done, he hated being called a "serial killer."

He believed once he was given a media-generated moniker, law enforcement treated him differently. He had been grouped into a category he felt he didn't belong in. Carl Patton was the infamous "Flint River Killer." Right up there with Son of Sam, the Zodiac Killer, and Ted Bundy.

Carl was known as the Flint River Killer because of where he disposed of his victims. But he hated that name, too. He said often, "I'm not a Ted Bundy."

To him, he saw a serial killer as someone who went after the same type of victim over and over and over. Carl was very clear that's not what he did. He didn't kill because of hair color, or stature, or because they were an easy target. He was adamant with me that every single person he killed he felt had done something to wrong to his family.

Norma agreed that's how her husband felt. "Oh yes, 100 percent."

He also felt that what was done to Melissa was just evil and out of retribution of some sort. Norma felt the same way. She believed Chris killed Melissa because he was mad at her, not his wife. "I didn't want them to get married. And I fought against the relationship as long as I could, and I just…he never…he would call me right after they got married and put Melissa on the phone and tricked me into saying something negative, then he would say, 'Melissa, do you hear what your momma just said?'"

I spoke with Tina and said straight out, "Your dad feels like he never killed an innocent person and that Melissa was an innocent person. She didn't do anything to another person to deserve what happened to her. She didn't take anybody's money. She didn't harm anybody. She didn't do anything that would result in somebody wanting to go after her in any way."

Tina replied, "He's right about that. Melissa was not a person that would do something wrong to somebody that somebody would have come up and say, 'Ah, well, you know, she stole all my money that I had in my house, so I'm going to take care of her.' She wasn't like that. She was quiet. She stayed to herself. She was not a troublemaker. Whatever trouble she had got into since she met Chris was because of Chris. He got her into trouble."

When I'm investigating a crime, I look for patterns. I look at blood patterns, handwriting, fingerprints, paying bills, text messages, work history, what time you leave for work, what time you get home from work, when you feed your dog, what church service you attend, what time you work out, what route you take to the grocery store, and criminal histories. I look at where, when, how, with who, and how often.

It's all patterns! All patterns that help tell a story of what happened and who did it. In Melissa's case, there was one pattern that was unmistakable and seemed to be pretty evident with everybody that we talked to: Melissa had a small circle. She hung out with her husband and her children and occasionally her mom and dad and, rarely, a coworker or two when she had a job. But she would also move from job to job. She and

Christopher frequently changed homes. Like Norma had said, Melissa often lived out of a suitcase. And it wasn't like she had these best friends who she would go hang out with or other associates of some sort. She didn't have that in her life. She was shy, kept to herself, only associated with family. Does this sound like a young woman who would up and leave for California to start a new life? Not a chance.

Chapter 10

GATHERING THE TEAM AND WALKING THE SCENE

IN MY BUSINESS, SOMETIMES IF you want to understand a killer or why somebody would kill, asking a killer is a good start. When I communicated with Carl, he told me what he thought happened to Melissa. He, as a man, said he understood her husband and what their relationship was and that the coward would always take things out on her.

Carl told me that he approached Christopher once and was "beating on him a little bit," and there was no pushback from him at all. Not surprising to Carl, when someone went toe-to-toe with Christopher, he would cower.

With the information Carl was providing, the investigation was moving into the suspectology phase. Suspectology is defined as a field of investigation focusing on understanding the mindset of potential suspects and then developing a picture by analyzing various aspects. Suspectology analyzes a suspect's behavior, history, and characteristics in order to build a comprehensive profile.

I knew Carl would be a tremendous asset in developing the suspectology on and gaining more insight into Christopher Wolfenbarger. Carl believed Christopher dumped the trash bags at Action Glass because he felt safe there at night. He knew no one would be around and if by chance someone stopped him, he was in the company work truck just doing business. He could have said he was dropping off equipment or returning the truck after a job ran long. But as Carl explained, no one would be around at 3:00 a.m., as an example. And Christopher would know that.

Carl and I agreed on another aspect of this case: We had to have a team. Just the two of us working the case was not going to yield an arrest, much less a conviction.

Carl asked me, "You think you and Karyn Greer could get folks caring about Melissa?"

Karyn Greer was one of Atlanta's top investigative reporters at WGCL/CBS 46. She also manned the anchor desk and was one of the area's most recognizable faces. She was exactly what we needed.

I told Carl that was exactly what I was going to do, and I knew how to do it. The only way to do it—show them!

Honestly, I think it was a miracle that Norma got the Henry County Police Department to even take a report. It wasn't in their jurisdiction. But at least they created a paper trail, and I appreciated that. It was good police work, but it was also fantastic outreach and advocacy.

I also appreciated the Henry County Police for the kindness they showed Norma. She had to show them the letters she had gotten from Melissa, and all the cards that Melissa had mailed her since she and Chris had gotten married. With those, Norma was able to prove that Melissa had stayed in contact with her to get them to take the report. It showed a clear and present pattern of contact.

The report, the investigation, would not have happened without Norma. She didn't give up. When they told her no, she went back.

Tina said about her mother, "You've got to have somebody that cares about the person to, you know...you've got to push. You can't just listen to them say no and walk away and say, 'Oh well.' You've got to push, and you have to push hard."

June 21, 2021, was one of those days that contributes to one of Atlanta's other nicknames—*Hot*lanta. It was more than hot. It was that kinda hot where you can see the heat coming off the street. But we had a mission. We wanted to show the crime scene to the new district attorney and investigator assigned to the case.

At the scene, we parked between where Melissa's skull had been found and the additional bags were located. Norma, Tina, and Tina's daughter, Kimberly, were in one car. Karyn Greer and her cameraman rode together in another car. Trace Sargent, founder and director of Forensic Investigations & Analysis Inc., and her K9s were in her truck; Dr. Duanne Thompson, associate professor of criminal justice, brought his equipment in his own car; and I was solo in my CSI truck. Both Trace and Duanne were volunteering their time and expertise like they'd done many times before. Serving where needed comes natural to them. Both are selfless, smart, loyal, and brave, and I'm proud to have them as part of my *Zone 7* podcast team.

Once the caravan had parked, Assistant District Attorney Adriane Love got out of the county vehicle driven by District Attorney Investigator Richard Stein. Adriane slowly approached me and asked that I introduce her to everyone. She took extra time with Norma. She then asked me to show her where the evidence was found.

Then she walked alone. I understood this need to walk it, feel it, absorb it. It was the best way to process what transpired there. As I stood there watching her work, Adriane walked from the skull location to the wood line, then back to where the skull was found. She then walked toward Action Glass, and when she turned around, I saw the look on her face. It was a look of determination and unbridled frustration.

Tina walked up to me and said, "She's mad."

Yep. She was. She was mad that this had gone on as long as it had. She was mad they lost so much valuable time. She was mad this case was cold.

She was mad because a young mother was taken from her babies. She was mad at a system that she had devoted her life to failed that young mother.

Adriane finally spoke. "How do you go from finding a skull in April to not finding the rest of the body parts till June? That's months that nothing is being done, and then when the person is misidentified, you lose four years of an investigation."

Sounded like Adriane got it. Norma and Tina smiled because they wanted her mad, and they appreciated her anger. They'd never had anyone on Adriane's level finally fighting for Melissa. Hopefully, that was about to change.

ADA Adriane Love was mad, and she wanted justice. She left that scene determined to put this case together for trial. I couldn't help but smile. We now had the assistant district attorney on board. We had Sergeant Layton from the Atlanta PD on board. We had Investigator Richard Stein on board. We had a serious dream team coming together.

Despite the heat, everyone was anxious to get started. Adriane watched Trace take her K9 out of the truck and start to work. If you've never seen a search K9 in action, it's something to behold. The dog paced back and forth, eager to be given more leash to go.

Suddenly, the dog took off into the thick woods, and Trace was engulfed by trees. Both she and her K9 partner were completely out of sight, totally concealed as they moved deeper into the invasive kudzu. Dr. Duanne Thompson gathered his high-tech metal detector and started searching the area for the saw used to dismember Melissa's body. Karyn Greer and her cameraman began setting up for a remote shot for their story on this new search for Melissa's torso and the potential tools or instruments used in her beheading and dismemberment.

Standing there at the crime scene, seeing these professionals and the best of the best doing their respective jobs, all for the sake of Melissa, I began to get a sense of the team. A true team that was finally on the same page about investigating her murder and putting all the pieces together. Norma felt it, too. She told me she finally felt like someone was going to do something. Someone was actually working toward bringing Melissa the justice she deserved.

I left the scene of the crime that first time knowing we were a lot closer than we'd ever been to catching the killer. As I said, when it comes to crime scenes, you can't substitute walking the scene. And you *sho Lord* can't substitute walking the scene with experts and family members of the victim! When I do, I get this all-encompassing view of who this person was, who loved them, what their life could have been, should have been.

When I walk a scene, I'm also looking to understand a number of key questions: Why this location? Who would know this road? Who traveled it often? Why *this* road? Why Avon Avenue? Why not a rural road? Who would have left Melissa here? Who would've felt comfortable enough to dump body parts in this location? Right here on Avon Avenue?

The suspect pool shrank dramatically because of Avon Avenue.

Chapter 11

KARYN GREER

MY FOURTH-GRADE TEACHER, MS. ELEANOR, had her husband take an old console TV, the kind that was housed in a wooden-framed cabinet, and remove the back panel, then clean out all the inner workings. He stripped out all the bulbs and wires of that old set. She then had him bring it to our classroom for us to use for our book reports. Literally, we got to do our book reports on TV! And for me, it was a complete game changer of whether I hated the idea of giving a book report or I couldn't wait to do it. For me, that weekly chore back in 1974 became something that I looked forward to. I was Mary Tyler Moore!

One thing we used to do as a family when I was a kid was watch *The Mary Tyler Moore Show.* My four sisters and I never missed an episode. We just loved the idea of being a news anchor. To me, they were so smart and fascinating because they knew all the news before anyone else. They were informative and, in an odd way, a friend. You trusted them and relied on them to let you know what was going on. They were celebrities.

Karyn Greer is part of my inner circle. Part of my team. That was like having the first-round draft pick! Karen thinks I taught her how to investigate, but it's not true. She has a gift that can't be acquired, given, or taught: People are drawn to her. I tell people all the time, and I've said it to her privately—as good as she is on TV, she's better one-on-one. When that camera is off, the way she truly loves and cares for people is amazing.

I used to tell people whenever they're watching some of those crime shows to understand the difference between fiction and reality. When a Hummer pulls up at a crime scene and a stiletto heel followed by a sexy leg slides out, it's probably fiction. I would tell them it's just not realistic—until I worked with Karyn Greer. She once came on a live scene in knee-high Gucci boots, and she worked the hell out of that scene. So now that I've seen somebody work a crime scene looking sexy, I figured I could never tell folks *that* again!

Karyn and I have worked many crime scenes together, but we worked Melissa Wolfenbarger from the ground up. Karyn will tell you she had those boots on because she was in between shows and had met me in the middle of her shift. We hung out for a couple of hours, and then she went back to the TV station and did another live hit.

She told me afterward, "I learned after that to bring other boots."

Karyn Greer shows up! She shows up for cases, stories, nonprofits, sorority events, and family—she just plain shows up! Karyn and I talk often at some of these crimes scenes we work together, and at some point we stop being a CSI and a news anchor and we're just two moms. She told me while working Melissa's case that she only saw a twenty-one-year-old young mom who needed someone to tell her story. Make the public see the horrific things that happened to her and know that her story was important.

Karyn covered this case for a long, long time. When she covers a case like this, according to Karyn, she tries to keep it fluid. "As you know, people will sometimes say, 'I saw something; I know something.' So, you don't want to ever discount some of those people who will contact you about your story because we have, as you know, heard from people who had a tidbit, had some information for us. So, I just try and keep it open and try and encourage people to be a part of our investigation. Work this with us, because it takes a village to solve some of these cases."

When it comes to investigations such as Melissa's, Karyn hits on an important facet of her role. A lot of times, people will talk to her when they won't talk to the police. The "Karyn Greer" that comes into their home every night—they *do* know her. They feel connected to her because they see her so much, listen to her point of view, and are familiar with the way she talks on TV.

In other words, they trust Karyn. Often, if someone doesn't trust law enforcement, Karyn has an in with them. And I think that's powerful. Karyn told me, "I've worked more than thirty years, three decades, in this market. And I've worked to be a trusted source, someone people felt comfortable talking to, that you weren't afraid of sitting down with me. That you knew that I was going to be fair and honest. So, I do love that."

Just like when we walked the crime scene where Melissa's dismembered body had been dumped, I love the way Karyn has guided me into walking crime scenes. You can't just say, "This happened in Southwest Atlanta." You need to go walk over there. See how it happened. See where the body was found. See where the house was, walk it, learn it, be a part of it, and I appreciate that.

I can honestly say, honey, there was no better time in my career than working with Karen Greer.

Once we made the decision we were going to take on the Melissa Wolfenbarger case, we made one of the smartest moves we could make, and it was critical to the investigation. We assembled everyone on the team—Norma and Tina, ADA Love, Investigator Stein, Dr. Thompson, and Trace and her K9s—right there at the crime scene, together. There was no confusion about where something happened, where something was located, what needed to be done next.

Everybody was there at the same time, on the same page, with one purpose: find additional evidence in the case of Melissa Wolfenbarger.

But something incredible happened when Adriane Love came on the scene.

As Karyn noted, "The ADA came in her work attire and walked into that wooded area looking for clues. She got in there, got dirty, and then, as she had a chance to talk to the family, the mother and sister, and told them, she's not letting this go. This is going to be something that she champions, because this case is just unbelievable."

Karyn and I both knew Adriane wasn't playing when it came to this case. And if anybody knew what was going on in Metro Atlanta right then, it was Adriane Love.

Karyn expressed a thought we all felt: "When everybody was there together and got to give their opinion about what should happen next and where we were with the case, and watching Duanne search for the saw... and just watching Trace work her dogs, I felt like we've got a really good chance of finding something, of locating something that might push this thing even further than we've gotten right now."

She added a fact that truly was amazing. "Those dogs with Trace, I've never seen anything like it. She got them out there on the scent. They charged into that wooded area—*charged*."

I was glad Investigator Richard Stein was there at the crime scene with us. It gave me the opportunity to explain my method of investigating a scene. I call it the 361 Vortex. You look up, you look down. You look to the left, you look to the right. You look in front of you, and you look behind you. You get down on the ground to see what bugs see. You rise above in a bucket truck to see what the birds see. You do a complete 360, and then you add one more.

Stein, like the rest of us, knew this was something for the playbook. There would be no waiting on an email or leaving a message on voicemail. While we were all there, each in our own professional capacity—this was where we would decide where we went next. *This*, the crime scene. And this was where we would go from ground zero to one, to two, to three, to four, and so on until we found the killer.

It reminded me of a friend I grew up with whose daddy, Gene Sutherland, ran a small business in Atlanta. Sutherland's Eggs. That small business became an incredibly large business, and it may have been due in part to Mr. Sutherland's way of thinking. He was famous for saying, "Let's have an understanding so we don't have a misunderstanding."

Good words to live by, and they came to mind while we were all still gathered there on Avon Avenue. There is so much technology now that none of us had back then. It just wasn't available. The state-of-the-art technology for the times was there now, though, and some of this evidence needed to be tested. We were all singularly focused on the next steps to solve this case and how each of us in our respective positions could contribute to bringing the justice Melissa deserved.

~

While each of us would play an important role, there was no doubt who would push it forward. The media is a tool for law enforcement on cold cases, period. The media can do things law enforcement just can't do and can reach a ton of people with one episode. I don't care whether it's a story on the nightly news, or a documentary, or something on social media.

Typically, your hometown newspaper or larger news organizations have more followers, viewers, and readers than the local police department. There's no better way to ask for the public's help with witnesses, a missing person, and other types of tips. You absolutely must have the media's help to reach the most people possible on cases, especially cold cases. As I've said, people often will speak to the media when they don't feel comfortable speaking to the police. I've seen it over and over. They know the reporter can't arrest them. They feel like they know that reporter personally, whereas they've never met that police officer asking them questions, making them hesitant to open up and talk about something they've seen or heard.

The media also has tools of their own, such as archives of past interviews and crime scene footage. This can be a money tree for law enforcement! As an investigator, if you can establish a good working relationship with a local reporter, you've hit the jackpot. You need crime scene footage from fifteen years ago? They've got it. Twenty-five years ago? They've got it, too. You may see a witness being interviewed who you didn't even know existed. Archived footage may contain a teacher or a neighbor or a boyfriend or girlfriend of the victim who's not in your file.

It also gives you the benefit of watching footage so you can see exactly what the scene looked like when the crime occurred. Whether it's been built up and that once empty lot has been developed, or if the woods have been cut down and now there's a building where the crime scene was. Or perhaps it's the opposite. That old cinder block mom-and-pop store is now deserted and overrun with brush and debris.

Law enforcement might have taken a video back then, but maybe they didn't, or maybe it's been lost. Maybe you haven't had time to convert it, so you don't have anything to watch it on if it's 8mm. Remember those? Your local news station can help you with that.

If you're in law enforcement, my advice is to nurture and protect your relationship with the media. You will need them one day. Just like I have needed Karyn all these years.

Chapter 12

TRACE

THE FIRST TIME I EVER saw a working dog I was four or five years old. A dog was helping a visually impaired lady cross Ponce de Leon in downtown Atlanta. As always, my mother took great care and concern explaining everything that dog was doing. Listening and watching for cars, watching for other people, making sure they had time to cross the street when the light changed. I was amazed. I mean, we had a dog, but he couldn't do any of that!

My mother explained that this dog was at work. It wasn't just a family pet but, literally, he had a job. I told her that I didn't know dogs could have jobs. She reminded me I'd seen dogs working on farms herding the other animals, and I'd seen dogs like Lassie in movies. She told me that our local jewelry store had a watchdog. That's their job.

Of course, I knew that dogs would sometimes search for and chase down escaped convicts, but my young mind was blown. I *did* know all those things to be true. I knew that dogs had jobs. I just never really thought about it like that. I certainly didn't know that they had jobs where they helped people.

In my career, I've been fortunate to work with dogs many, many times. Canines searching for missing elderly, lost children, dope, firearms, bombs, and, of course, an escaped prisoner or two. I've seen, in person, canines that responded to the Olympic Park bombing in Atlanta and the 9/11 terror attacks. I've even seen the difference these incredible creatures have made in the lives of those suffering by providing therapy in their gentle manner. Dogs can even help identify medical issues like alerting somebody to a seizure before it happens.

I've been lucky enough in my job to have watched Trace Sargent at work more than once. When I say work, I mean *work!* A house now sits where a junkyard used to be across the street from Action Glass. We have searched for evidence behind that home for a saw or Melissa's torso. Trace ran her dogs all around the house. We did not find anything associated with this case. She went down to South Georgia for me on a missing person case. We have worked a murder case searching for evidence in the woods. We've even worked a Dixie Mafia case together.

Trace has never told me no when I've called and asked for her help. Never. Her dogs are expertly trained. They need water. They need food. They need vests. Her car needs gasoline. She needs food and water herself. And she has never asked me for anything. In every case we've worked together over the years, she's done it on a volunteer basis.

Although Trace has her PhD in psychology, she's a master at understanding animal behavior. And she's not limited to dogs. She has all sorts of animals trained and ready for their screen debuts. Need a turtle for a movie? She's got one. A goat? Got one of those, too. How about a bird? Her feathered friend may look like a diva, but it's just acting. And it's all in the training. Next time you see an animal in a movie, hang around for the credits. It may be one of hers.

I've had the privilege of watching Trace and her K9 lay tracks before. It's a sight to see. Trace explains the science behind using the dog's natural instinct. She says, "If you think of the concept of a rabbit or a deer, it's the dog's natural drive to hunt down the prey instead of a predatory animal like a wolf or a coyote that will down a rabbit or deer to kill it and eat it. Dogs have those same instincts and drives. We just channel those drives differently."

She describes laying tracks as giving the dog something to follow. She used me as an example. "I would say, Sheryl, I need you to lay a track for me. So you would go one hundred yards, turn right, go a couple hundred more yards, turn left, and then go about a hundred more yards and hide somewhere. The dog is then turned loose to 'follow your track.'"

Trace says exercises like laying tracks is all part of the dogs' training, their maintenance, and their conditioning. Trace likes to give credit where credit is due. "I really can't take much credit for these dogs, and I've learned that over the years. We just channel those natural drives these dogs already have. They really have superpowers. And after all the years I've been doing this, it's still like magic watching them work. It truly is incredible how effortless and how happy these dogs are when they do the work that we ask them to do."

Trace has worked bomb dogs in Iraq. She's worked specially trained service dogs that help people with physical challenges and disabilities. She's worked farm dogs. Still, people know her best as a subject-matter expert in missing person cases, both dead and alive. Trace has worked with numerous agencies over the years, and her name will usually come up when they're putting together any type of team.

Cop killers, rapists, murderers…you name it, her dogs have run it down. Trace has worked with so many families over the years, she'll tell you, "It doesn't matter who they are, where they come from, why their loved one is missing. What matters is that the not knowing is the absolute worst life that these people can live."

Even with all the training, seminars, podcasts, and expert guest appearances she had on her schedule, she didn't hesitate when I called her about Melissa's case.

From the very beginning of Melissa's case, I knew I wanted Trace on the team. Karyn Greer and I talked over and over about who we should bring in on this first grouping. And I wanted an eclectic group, but I wanted a group that I knew would gel and be on the same page from the start. Trace Sargent was a must-have.

And when she pulled up in her big ol' red truck, you could already hear the dogs barking. They knew they were going to work, and they were excited about it. Trace had her vest on, she had the dogs' water, she had everything they needed. Like the dogs, she was ready to go. And yet she took time to speak to everybody, to make sure she understood the layout. She asked the right questions: Where do you think this happened? Where was this found? Where was that found? When her dogs are alerting and pulling her somewhere, she wants to understand why. She wants it to make sense. It's like watching an Olympic ice-skating couple going for the gold. Trace Sargent and her dogs are so in sync, it's beyond a partnership. She understands exactly what they're doing and where they're headed.

At Melissa's crime scene, Trace never missed a beat or a step despite the first dog pulling her into the woods. And the woods get mighty thick in Georgia during the summertime. Jungles of kudzu take over everything. And you need a hatchet to move through the briars and thickets. But that dog just disappeared, and Trace disappeared right behind him. It was like nothing I'd ever seen in my life. It was like the woods just swallowed them whole. Although I couldn't see them, I could hear the dog. I could hear Trace. And then silence. I didn't hear anything for a long time. Finally, they both emerged out of the woods.

As Trace got ready to run the second dog, she shared a heartbreaking story. "I've had a number of dogs over the years. If we go back to the Natalee Holloway case, which happened many years ago. I was still living in Alabama at the time. And long story short, I was on a case in Georgia and it was for a nine-year-old girl that had been missing for, I think, over twenty years.

"But that day changed my life. And that was the case where Logan, looking for her remains, had actually slipped down a very steep embankment and he went to the edge of the road and as a car came around, it hit him in the head and killed him instantly. It really, really hit me hard, because these dogs are more than just team members to me. They're family."

The sorrow of losing the dog was compounded by the feeling she had failed him. "I just felt that day that I failed him. He never failed me. He always protected me. He always protected my life, because I trusted him 100 percent, and that just…it took me awhile to get over that one. But I also learned from my experience with Logan—I will never, ever be without at least two, sometimes three working dogs at any one time."

From an investigative standpoint, when you work two dogs and both dogs go to the same area and alert, and both dogs are giving you the same information, then that's just a money tree. Two noses are better than one. Not to say that one dog is better than the other, but it does help not only from an investigative point of view, but also from a prosecution point of view to say that this wasn't just an anomaly; this wasn't just one dog having an interesting day, but we have not only one, but two, and now three confirmed hits in the same area.

Trace continues: "But what I've actually learned, and I would say that has changed in my strategic approach to these cases—not only from the dog's perspective, but also from an investigative perspective as far as how I approach different areas—is that detection dogs don't find bombs, bodies, and drugs for us. But wait…isn't that what they're trained to do? Aren't they trained to find drugs and bombs and people? No. They're trained to find *scents*. My mindset, when I'm searching in different areas in different cases and different times of the year, I don't look at it from the perspective of, yes, okay, where would a body be or where would this be, but where would the scent be.

"And scent behavior changes throughout the day. Search in the early morning, scent conditions can be very, very different, especially here in the South in the summertime and it's very hot and humid. Scent in the middle of the day is almost nonexistent because the hot sun and the heat literally vaporizes it. It literally kills any scent.

"There's a rhyme and a reason of why we use these dogs in certain areas at certain times of the day in certain times of the year. A great example of that is when we're working with archaeology projects. These are typically the Civil War, the Revolutionary War, and other types of wars that happened 150, 200, 300 years ago. We never work those scenes in the heat. Not because the dogs can't do it, but because the scent just isn't there. They can't pick up a scent if it doesn't exist. So, when we work these old historical projects or even cold cases, the time of the day and the time of the year does matter, not because of the abilities of the dog, but because of the behavior of the scent."

On Melissa's case, I was hoping we would have the dogs alert on the torso. That was the one part of her body that hadn't been found.

I knew if any two dogs could do it, it would be Trace's. As I watched her dogs work, it fascinated me to see how they kept their noses to the ground 90 percent of the time. But there were a couple of times their noses would go straight up in the air. Trace explained that on that particular day, although we started early in the morning, we did spend some time speaking with the family and one another. As we were talking, the scent conditions changed a little bit.

"When you see fog in the morning, it's down in the lower valleys," Trace said. "And if you actually watch fog as the day heats up, the fog actually lifts up."

That's a great analogy and a great example of what human scent, especially cadaver scent, does. It settles into the lower valleys during the evening, and as the heat of the day rises, so does the scent. Trace adds, "When you see those different behaviors in a dog as far as their nose on the ground or nose up in the air, they're telling us a story. And that's where my mind must step in in this partnership. This dog is telling us a story, and what is that story telling us?"

When a dog alerts, or "hits" as some people call it, it's because they've picked up a human scent in the area. Trace explains as a dog handler, in her mindset, part of the job is not only putting the dog in the right place at the right time but also reading the information and the story that's telling us. "And part of that story is change of behavior, or what we call COB." Trace says over the years, she recognized in herself that she was too focused on the alert. "My dogs are trained to sit when they find a scent. That's their trained alert behavior. When I first started this, I was too focused on that behavior. Is he going to sit? Is he going to sit? Is he going to sit? But through maturity and experience, I realized that's not the most important thing. The most important thing is reading the whole story.

"So when we have a change of behavior, that to me is just as important, because scent sometimes—especially in these really old cases like Melissa's—can be so fickle and so faint, that that slightest change of behavior, the rise of the dog's head or the change in the direction in his nose or his tail or something, that in itself, may be the only thing the dog does that gives me some hint he may be picking something up."

For me, it's so important to recognize that change in behavior. I hammer and hammer and hammer patterns, patterns, patterns, and as soon as somebody breaks the pattern, that's my first red flag. It's vital to know the opposite is also true; it could also be a positive thing.

At Melissa's scene, the dogs were telling us all kinds of things, and nothing was going to be negative. There was no failure on that day. The dogs did tell us something—they told us where the evidence *wasn't*. That, to me, was powerful.

It was hot, and Trace was wearing her full uniform, and she was working these dogs, running in and out of the woods, in and out of briars, up and down steep and rocky terrain that was difficult to traverse. At the end of it, she had run two dogs for I don't know how long. She had already walked the scene herself to familiarize herself with it. She had to have been physically exhausted.

Despite the exhaustion, Trace took the time to talk to Norma. She explained exactly what they had done, exactly what the dogs told her, and exactly what they were capable of and weren't capable of. Just watching Trace with Melissa's momma, I understood the part of running a canine most people don't know about and probably never witness—talking to the family.

Trace says, "When I'm working with any officials and even with family members, I can only promise them one thing. At the end of the day, we will know more than we did at the beginning of this day. And these dogs, they tell us two things. They tell us where something is and they tell where something isn't. It's extremely rare that we take the dogs to an area and we find what we're looking for right away. It happens, and we're always excited when that happens, but it's rare."

I've learned over the years that knowing where something isn't can be just as important, if not even more important, than knowing where something is. And most of these cases are not about the proverbial smoking gun. It's about just dogged perseverance, determination, not giving up, leaving no stone unturned, and checking every place, even if it's not a high-priority area. At least we can mark it off the list. It's never a waste of time. It's never a negative thing.

We now knew more about Melissa's case than we did the day before, and we knew she was not here. Her remains weren't here, and what we were looking for was not here, and we could move on from that now. These dogs are so much: They are a partner. They are a teammate. They are a tool, but they're also investigators. And like so many investigators out there, they may go to hundreds of scenes and nothing comes of it. But it's always that one time. This could be that one day.

Trace says it best. "Whether you're getting paid for this, whether you're volunteering your time, it doesn't matter. These families deserve the very best I can give to them. These dogs—the families deserve the very best that these dogs can give them. And I approach every case that way because the families deserve that. I have worked cases where we did find a person's loved one, and we immediately have to come out and we have to give the death notification. And it's extremely emotional. The grieving, the screaming, the hitting, the punching, the denial, the anger, the…just the heartache…all of that.

"At the same time, I'd rather have that any day than what I did in Melissa's case. And I've done it so many times. It doesn't get any easier, because you can see the expression on their face when they…there's just something about a dog and it's like, 'Oh, look, it's Rin Tin Tin, it's Lassie!' It's all of these kind of heroic things, and these dogs really do have superpowers. For the families to see the dog and get out of the vehicle, it's almost like, 'Oh finally! Finally, they're going to give the answers we so, so desperately need and deserve.'

"It's a lot of responsibility. I'd rather have the screaming and the hurting and the pain of a death notification than I would walking out of the woods and looking at Melissa's family or any other family member and saying, 'I'm sorry; I wish I could give you answers. I do have answers for you, but we haven't found your loved one yet.' And it's just…it's heartbreaking for them. It really is. My heart hurts for them."

Trace shares a sentiment we all feel in law enforcement. "The reality is, a lot of these cases do become cold, and not to say that they're not important, but there's only so much law enforcement can do. It's really heartbreaking that these families think nobody cares anymore. And I just want them to know that, yes, people still care. And, God willing, as long as I can physically do this and the dogs can physically do this, we're going to continue searching for Melissa and any of those other missing persons as long as we can."

Because of what Trace did on that day, it helped me formulate a theory of what I thought happened to the torso. And the fact she didn't find it helped me solidify what I believed, and I think that spoke to the killer and the killer's mindset at the time. My friend Todd Pitchford, who is a detection dog expert with Detection Dogs of America, always says, "Trust your dog."

Chapter 13

THE BEST OF THE BEST

AT THE NACOLE SMITH COLD case and crime scene, specifically, I remember Karyn and I had the conversation that, at some point, she stops being a news anchor and I stop being a crime scene analyst and we're just two mommas. Karyn and I both knew Melissa's story wasn't going to be an easy one to tell, but it needed to be told. She was only twenty-one years old and the mother of two small children, both still in diapers. Karyn had to craft a story to compel action, not just from police and prosecutors and experts but the public at large.

This was not an easy sell. It was a family where the parents had been involved in committing homicides themselves, and now we were asking people to care about what happened to their child despite their past. If anyone could do it, Karyn Greer could.

I knew she'd reflect the love, concern, and care for Melissa in a way that would generate empathy. Karyn would make the tragedy of Melissa's death so apparent that people would understand what happened to her was a separate matter from her parents' crimes. It needed to be looked at because someone was walking around free. A killer who had beheaded and dismembered a twenty-one-year-old mother of two. And we knew that Melissa, through no fault of her own, was born into the Patton family. She had nothing to do with the sins of her parents.

The cruel way she was murdered, dismembered, beheaded, placed in trash bags, and thrown out like garbage was unforgivable. Karyn said, "It was important for us to tell that story so that people didn't blame her, didn't look at her family situation as a reason why no one cared. You have to care. Look at her smile. Look at her innocence. You look at her babies' faces, who are not babies now because this has been so long. And it just breaks your heart."

Carl Patton wrote a letter to me and Karyn. In that letter, he told us up until Melissa's murder, he had no idea what he'd done to the families of his victims. He was young and stupid and never considered how his actions would affect those who loved the people he'd killed. He never realized how he'd destroyed their worlds. He wrote that every day since he found about what had happened to his baby daughter, he'd felt the sorrow of a grieving parent, and remorse and guilt for what he'd done years ago.

When another murderer, Scott Peterson, was talking to Diane Sawyer in 2003, he said something interesting about his missing wife, Laci: She was amazing. That one key word: *was*. He referred to her in past tense. That was so important for law enforcement. If he was referring to her in past tense, he, on some level, didn't believe she was coming home. What would make him believe that? Score a big one for the media.

There are people in the media who have done unbelievable work on cases. We all know Bob Woodward and Carl Bernstein and what they did when it came to Watergate. It led, in part, to the resignation of the president of the United States. Karyn Greer has put cases out there, too, that ended with positive conclusions. Part of the reason they did is because Karyn would not let these cases go. She was going to keep them in the spotlight. Cases like Honey Malone, Nacole Smith, and, of course, Melissa Wolfenbarger.

Karyn said, "In three decades here in Atlanta; Charleston, South Carolina; Champaign, Illinois—I've never seen anything to this degree. It's amazing, the twists and turns in this case that make it so intricate. But it's going to get solved."

I knew that media was going to be a big part of Melisa's case. It would keep it alive. Melissa's case wasn't on anybody's radar. She hadn't been a celebrity or gone missing at a tropical resort. No one was talking about

Melissa Wolfenbarger. Nobody was doing anything about it. Nobody was mad about it. Enter Karyn Greer, and that whole thing changed.

We got the opportunity to go with Nancy Grace to CrimeCon and discuss Melissa's case live. Professionals with so much knowledge and experience were eager to help, including famed FBI agent and member of the Behavioral Analysis Unit Jim Clemente and Jared Bradley with the DNA collection firm M-Vac.

Carl later told me, "That's what it takes. Now people can't ignore all of you. Not now that Nancy Grace has talked about Melissa. That's a criminal organization tactic. Put the best and most trusted people in the highest places so you can make maximum moves." Carl was right again, so I added an extra expert.

When Karyn and I worked the Nacole Smith case, we had the chance to work with famed investigator Paul Holes. We asked his opinion on Melissa's case, and he gave it freely. Now that was a *maximum move*!

All these people giving the best of themselves was, to me, such an uplifting part of what we do. In fact, I get asked a lot: "How do y'all not burn out?"

How do you burn out when you're surrounded by heroic, brilliant, and loving people willing to give so much of themselves to help others? It's an honor to get to work with them every day. Not a day goes by when we don't have the opportunity to help, save, and restore lives. We fight to bring justice to someone who can no longer fight for themselves without fear or favor. *That's* an honor.

Sergeant Raymond Layton is an incredible ambassador for the Atlanta Police Department. Just a spectacular human being. But aside from that, he's capable, willing, and ready to jump in with both feet every chance he gets. He's also open and willing to listen when somebody asks if we've tried such and such or can help connect us to somebody who can open doors to some new technology.

There's a common denominator with my career and the way I work cases: Get everybody in on it! Get teachers, plumbers, actors, detectives, preachers all in the same room working on the same case at the same time, trying to help a family get answers. When there are experts, survivors, authors, podcasters, and media personalities all in the same place for the same reason, it is an unbelievable experience.

Vince Velazquez is a retired homicide detective in Atlanta and is now on the hit TV series *ATL Homicide*. He has volunteered with the CCIRI for the past twenty years, and we have worked on numerous cases together. Vince told me years ago that if anybody contacts him and says they have an idea for how he can solve a case, his only response should be "thank you" and mean it.

We are all trying our best to solve these cases, but maybe, just maybe, another detective, CSI, or prosecutor sees a way to solve it. Or even a civilian. I tell people all the time: I do not have a crystal ball. Trust me, I would use it if you gave it to me. If you have an idea, I'm ready to hear it and, if possible, try it. Vince even said about the Nacole Smith case, "I'm retired, but I will work this case for free till the day I die!"

I know people sometimes have negative things to say about law enforcement. People have negative things to say about the media. But I can honestly tell you that has never been my experience. I have seen extraordinary work from amazing people in law enforcement and the media who only want to help.

Karyn and I have partnered on stories that resulted in winning an Emmy. We've been nominated three times with one win, so twice the voters got it wrong. I have called Karyn night or day and said, "Look, I want to tell you something, but it's got to be off the record." Never once has she violated her ethics or our friendship in search of a story. She has never hurt a family. She has never shoved a microphone in somebody's face who was falling apart and having the worst moment of their life. When it comes to Karyn Greer, I've only seen integrity, love, and compassion and needing to get the information out, needing to tell the story. Atlanta news is better because she is in it. The state of Georgia is better because she's in it. And I know these cold cases have a greater opportunity to see a conclusion when Karyn is involved. Families feel like they finally have a voice because of Karyn.

Stephanie Bauer, true-crime reporter for *People* magazine, says, "Always remember, these stories belong to the families. All we can do for them and the loved one they've lost is to tell the story. It's for the families. And when the teleprompter keeps rolling, just speak from the heart."

Melissa Wolfenbarger didn't have a team in life, but she had a dream team working for her in death. I was able to pull together the best of the best. Working together, I knew in my heart we'd find Melissa's killer.

Chapter 14

LETTERS FROM CARL

MS. ELEANOR, MY FOURTH-GRADE TEACHER, surprised us one day by giving us each the name and address of a child in Denmark. She told us that we were going to have a pen pal that whole school year, and we were going to write letters to them every week. At Christmastime, we were going to exchange gifts. We were going to know their birthday and other special times for them so we could send them a gift or some type of special recognition.

That was a wonderful experience for me because once I mailed off my letter, the anticipation of getting one in return was always such a blast. I couldn't wait for my pen pal to write me back. But it was a painstakingly slow process. It was different from making a phone call where you got immediate answers to your questions like, What's your favorite toy? Do you play a sport? Do you have brothers and sisters? We had to wait weeks to find out those answers.

I had that same experience with another pen pal—Carl Patton.

By the time it was confirmed that his baby daughter had been murdered, Carl had been imprisoned for fourteen years. Even from behind bars, he wanted to be a part of seeking justice for Melissa. *I* wanted Carl to be a part of the investigation because I knew his openness and honesty about being a killer himself was rare. Learning how many of his fellow inmates committed crimes, fled, covered up, avoided detection, and ultimately got caught is rare insight we don't normally get. And it was an opportunity I didn't want to pass up.

For me, that kind of added awareness would only increase my insight into Melissa's case as well as my depth of understanding for future cases. After working with Carl, getting to know the man, and the killer, it was clear that he was literally helping every single family that would come after. Every father grieving a murdered daughter, or a mother questioning why, or a detective asking how—Carl could help. That's a powerful and unexpected legacy.

This case was like no other in history, and I'm not saying that lightly. I have never worked a case or even had a buddy who has worked a case like this. I've never read about another case like it. I can't find a case like it on the internet. I can't even find anything in just *general research* that has happened like this.

In Melissa Wolfenbarger's case, we have a serial killer turned crime victim, who then turned to the detective who had arrested him for help, who then turned to a nonprofit for help, and who then got his family to meet with the district attorney about his daughter's case. Carl tried to put as much effort into finding his daughter's killer as he possibly could from where he sat in prison. With the limited resources available to him, he was still able to provide the most important tool to the investigation—his mind. The mind of a killer.

If you want to know why people murder, ask a murderer. Carl had information that I needed, and the only way I could get it was the old-fashioned way—through letters. I couldn't just pick up the phone and call him. I couldn't sit down with him and pick his brain over a cup of coffee. I couldn't grill Carl on my podcast, *Zone 7*. He didn't have access to a computer with headphones or a cell phone. He was not allowed outside visitors that were not family members. I made a formal request to the Department of Corrections to meet with him, and I was denied.

I often tell students and rookies that the art of letter writing is going away. Students don't know how to write in cursive. They abbreviate everything. And they can't *read* cursive, so historical documents are virtually useless to them for background and knowledge. It's scary to think we'll soon have a workforce that can't read the Constitution, old letters and wills, draft cards, death notices, and other important documents. They'll be powerless to research their own family history in full, let alone older cold cases.

Carl has beautiful cursive handwriting. Fortunately, I can read it.

I felt like it was important to include several of Carl's letters in this book. I wanted to share his handwriting, word selection, and phrasing. I wanted to share the goofy little drawings he added in his closings. The letters show the way he writes, the patterns, his feelings, his beliefs, and his sorrowfulness.

For years, Carl and I communicated through these handwritten letters. We communicated about his life growing up when he was a little boy. I've asked him intimate questions about his family, his crimes, his incarceration, and his fight for justice for Melissa.

Carl Patton murdered five people in cold blood. He never denied that to me. He didn't deny it in court, either. After his arrest in 2003, he walked into three separate courtrooms and admitted what he had done. Not a single case went to trial. And for his crimes, Carl deserved to be in prison.

He never misrepresented the facts to me, that I know of. I've read every court transcript but the one from Fayette County. And the only reason I haven't read that one is because under the Freedom of Information Act, they wanted thousands of dollars for the copies.

Every question I ever asked Carl, he answered, sometimes more than once. He was gracious and open with his answers, thoughtful with his questions, and sometimes he was just downright funny.

The first letter I received from him was dated March 4, 2021. He started the letter by stating, "Nearly 23 years ago, Melissa Dawn was stolen from her two children and family that loves her very much."

It struck me that he used present tense to express that they loved her. My mother-in-law does the same thing when she speaks about my father-in-law who died several years ago. Her love for him is in the present and still active. I remember my own mom telling me after my father died that when she took her vows about richer or poorer and until death do us part, she said, "I was not just talking about his life but mine, too. She was going to be married to him until she died."

Carl was baffled why no one was in prison for the murder of his child. In the same letter, he stated clearly, "I know guys in prison doing life that have less against them!"

I couldn't disagree with that statement. And there was a ton of circumstantial evidence in this case.

Carl believed that Chris's sister, Kimberely, and mother, Kathy Wolfenbarger, helped to cover up the crime or at least knew what he had done. Carl said he remembered shopping one day with Norma when they ran into Kimberely. Norma asked her if she had seen Melissa. In the letter, Carl wrote that Kimberely "started crying."

To me, that behavior clearly suggested that Kimberely knew something more than she has ever told. Why would she start crying if she believed Melissa went to start a new life in California? Why was she not angry with Melissa for abandoning her brother and their children?

In his second letter dated April 21, 2022, Carl gave a classic Carl Patton statement: "I would like to ask Ms. Adriane not to seek the death penalty on Chris but, life without parole, to give him time to think and realize what he done to his children and grandchildren by not knowing their mother and grandmother."

Carl's letters came on a regular basis, and I found myself looking forward to them. I wanted justice for Melissa as badly as her family did.

> *June 16, 2021*: Ms. Sheryl, I would like to correct something you said in your letter. You said Chris knew that I'd kill him if I ever got out. Norma made me promise I wouldn't, not out of forgiveness, but for the sake of the children and Melissa's grandson, and the fact that I would be back in prison. Sheryl, Chris is not worth me being separated from my family one more minute. Plus, I really did not understand the hurt and grief I caused with my

actions until we lost Melissa. I never want to cause anyone that type of pain ever again, and I pray God has or will forgive me for my sins and actions.

April 21, 2022: I am anxious about the evidence that has been found. My main focus is on the bags Melissa's body was placed in. We both know it would be hard to tie knots, especially in plastic bags, without leaving trace evidence of some sort. Whenever murder occurs, some kind of evidence is left no matter how careful the killer is. Evidence will be there. It may be overlooked, but that does not mean it's not there. There is no perfect crime. P.S. I told Norma and Tina Mae I was glad you and Ms. Adrian were never after me when I was doing wrong. Thank God I am not that man any longer.

July 22, 2022: Melissa Dawn was my baby girl who carried my heart the first time I held her. She was a happy, beautiful young lady. Made good grades in school, was in JROTC, and had the bright future in front of her. All that changed when she met Chris Wolfenbarger. He had an unhealthy influence on her. She changed, and not for the better. She started sneaking out at night to meet him and do God knows what. He even talked her into stealing my car twice. She and Chris had planned to run away to California—his idea. After Melissa became pregnant and had Christina, Chris done everything he could to keep Melissa and Christina away from me and Norma. Now, she had to sneak away from him, not sneak to meet him. The only time we ever got to see Melissa and Christina was when Chris was at work. Melissa told us that she'd be in big trouble if he found out. She often had bruises on her arms and neck. Norma and I tried to tell her it was an unsafe and unhealthy relationship, but she was in love and wouldn't listen. When Melissa didn't show up at Christmas to get her gifts and then we couldn't locate her, I knew in my mind and heart, Chris had done something to Melissa.

September 16, 2022: Ms. Sheryl, thank you for taking time out of your busy schedule to write and continue to keep me informed on Melissa's case. Last week was a rough one. Melissa would have turned 45 on Friday. Your letters are greatly appreciated. They continue to reassure me that someone other than my family is concerned in seeking justice for her. Thank you for your effort and determination on Melissa's behalf. My family and I owe a great debt of gratitude that cannot be repaid.

October 11, 2022: How do you kill the mother of your two children, and when you look at those children in the eye and say, your mother deserted you because she didn't want you. Then when it's proven this mother is dead and they want us to visit the grave, you take them to a different location and claim someone must have moved her. Ms. Sheryl, I have told you I had to lose Melissa and feel the pain to really realize the damage and harm I caused people I did not know. Please tell me, who does Chris have to lose to realize the hurt, heartache, and anguish his actions caused? A guilty conscience is a hell on earth that continues to punish and convict, and I deal with it every day. I pray that one day soon, Chris will get a conscience and see the wrong he has done. I wish Chris had killed me instead of Melissa. That way, I wouldn't have to live with the guilt of knowing I was not there to protect her. Every time I look at her picture, pain is the price

> you pay for loving your children so deeply. I want you to know my family and I appreciate your efforts in Melissa's case and keeping us in the loop. Chris Wolfenbarger has gotten away with his crime long enough. And, for the first time in a long time, I believe he will get his due very soon. Also, pleased to see the investigating agents agree with me that there is only one suspect in this case, Chris Wolfenbarger. Have read the geographic profile several times and, for the most part, I agree 95 percent. I want you to know, in my heart, killer does not describe me. Loving, protective father, husband, and provider describe me, and I pray you will see that as well. I'm willing to do anything to help bring Melissa's killer to justice. I have only two goals left in my life. One is justice for Melissa and getting back home to my family to hear my children's laughter and to wake up next to my wife one more time. This is my dream.

~

When I first reviewed the case file, I saw so much good work had been done once they identified Melissa's remains and knew she was a murder victim. But one thing I saw that was missing was a geographical profile.

A geographical profile is really an extraordinary and just supercool tool for law enforcement. The investigators putting the profile together take all the locations that are connected to either a crime or a series of crimes, and they try to determine the most probable area where an offender can be placed. This map will show a location that is most likely where the offender's base is. That base is either his home or his work. In other words, it's somewhere he knows intimately. He feels safe. He feels protected. He feels like he could carry out his crime or crimes from there very easily.

The investigators then analyze a string of locations that could be connected to the crime. It's most likely where this person traveled, the route they took after they committed the crime. If you have somebody who leaves their home, interacts with a victim, murders that victim, and then dumps the body somewhere, this establishes the geographical profile. When investigators know the body disposal site and where the victim was last seen, they'll work backwards to establish the most likely area where the perpetrator lived or worked.

Many elements are used to load the information into the analysis and mapping. Was the victim found outdoors? In an abandoned building? In their home? On a street somewhere? After that, they're going to utilize witness statements, law enforcement reports, and get that exact address of where the victim was last seen. That gives investigators two critical points: Where the body was located, and where the victim was last seen.

They also include aspects from the victim's life in the geographical profile. Where the victim went to school, where the victim worked. Where did this killer and victim first intersect? Law enforcement can try to predict that. When looking at a map, there's going to be hot zones where the victim crosses into where the perpetrator may live. Maybe every day she passes where he works to go to her own job, or her school, or her church, or wherever it was that she was headed.

Then we move to the principle elements: Where did she live? Where did she work? Where were her parents, her siblings, et cetera?

One of the best geographical profilers I know is Douglas MacGregor. We had a series of crimes in Atlanta not too long ago, and as soon as I heard about them, I knew they sounded oddly familiar. It was kind of like a déjà vu thing. I couldn't understand why the crimes sounded so familiar when they were unfolding right then. I reached out to David Quinn, who was the detective on the crimes that I was remembering. I asked him if the new crimes sounded like the cases he'd worked previously. The first thing that crossed my mind was a copycat. Could *this* be a copycat? David agreed they sounded similar. And that it could be a copycat.

I contacted Douglas, and in real time and real quick from his office in Canada, he did a profile. To my amazement, he said it wasn't a copycat. This was a stranger. He said this perpetrator had no idea of the other crimes we were talking about, and he was going to strike in the general area always. Everything Douglas sent me, I sent to the sergeant handling the case, and it turned out he was absolutely right.

When I asked Douglas if he would possibly look at Melissa Wolfenbarger's case, he never hesitated. He generated a report stating she had most likely been killed at one location and then transported and discarded at another. I passed the report along to the police and the prosecutor. The geographical profile added yet another tool to Melissa's case that had never been used before. It was one more piece of information we could give to investigators and the DA's office. We could hand it over and truthfully say it wasn't just us telling them these things; here was an analysis being done by an expert in another country that's going to show you the same thing.

> *November 3, 2022:* In your last letter, you also asked very pointed questions about my past, family, Norma, parents, children, and crimes, things that are usually off-limits. However, I'm going to try to answer them as honestly as I can. So I will start at the beginning. My mother, my father, lived through The Great Depression and know what it meant to work hard and still do without. My dad used to tell me when you needed a new pair of shoes, all you had to do was put a piece of cardboard in the bottom of the old ones. Was his second son and only one of my mother, whom was 36 years old when I came along. Mom was the oldest girl of eight, and had to help watch after her other brothers and sisters. She always dreamed of having her own children, but I came late in their lives. Family

rumor says she found out she was pregnant. She ran around yelling, I got me a hot shot, and that's where I got my nickname, and nothing to do with my criminal activities. Mom and Dad always made sure I knew I was loved, wanted, and protected. Growing up I liked to play football and fish. Did not like school. My mother was always my safety blanket and my best friend. That's why it hurts now to know I disappointed her sometimes, and another reason I'm trying now to be a better person. Family loyalty started with my grandfather. He always said, family first, and to be true to your word and your friends. He taught my mother, and she taught me. Now, I try to pass that on to my children. All my mother ever wanted was for me to go to church, get educated, own my own home, and have grandchildren. She loved Norma. And the happiest I ever saw my mother was when Norma gave birth to our first daughter. After Tina Mae was born, Norma could do no wrong. Wait. I'm getting ahead of myself. When I was young and growing up, we lived in College Park. My grandfather Patton lived on Main Street in a two-story, three-bedroom mansion he built from a two-room shack. He was a master carpenter. Long about 1961, we moved to Ellenwood, east of Forest Park. Mom had rented 406 acres of land and a two-bedroom house for $60 a month. No heat. Used coal heaters and a fireplace to stay warm, where I honed my hunting skills, when my mom bought my first house there, I met the Wade sisters, Donna and Teresa. The three of us rode horses every day after school. We all attended Jonesboro Junior High School where I made some lifelong friendships. My happiest days had begun. Teresa Wade introduces me to my future. There she was, dark complexion, pretty smile, brown eyes and gray hair—not a lot of gray hair, but

> enough to be interesting at 15 years old. There she stood, my soulmate, lifelong partner, best friend, lover, mother, rock of my future family, Norma.

~

On August 15, 2022, Carl received a letter from the State Board of Pardons and Parole that stated, "The Board has considered your case in accordance with Board policy and denied parole."

Carl wanted to be home. He wanted and needed to be around his family. He told me on several occasions that he didn't think he had many years left and wanted to spend what time he had with his loved ones.

> *August 17, 2022*: God forgives the Parole Board doesn't.

Carl was a man trapped. Caged. He had no outlet to help bring justice to his child. He couldn't search, fight, or investigate. He had to wait hour upon hour, day by day, and month by month. The years stacked up on him like garbage in a landfill. He often didn't see a way out. He did all the system had asked of him. He took classes, graduated from programs, helped new inmates learn the rules and system, stayed out of trouble, and all for what? They were never going to let him out. He was, after all, the Flint River Killer. He literally spent nearly thirty years unable to do what he instinctively needed to do—protect his family.

Chapter 15

NOT ON MY WORST ENEMY

I HAVE OFTEN BEEN ASKED if Melissa's murder was some type of retribution for Carl's murders. If it was, why wait twenty-one years to get revenge? I reached out to the children of one of Carl's last victims, Liddie Evans, in hopes they'd speak with me about their mother. I invited them to be a guest on my podcast, *Zone 7*. The children, now adults, would have the opportunity to honor their mother, and we'd have the chance to look deeper into Carl's crimes. I was anxious to see if his crimes factored into the murder of his own daughter.

As a family, we knew Uncle Clark, my mother's favorite uncle, was a thief, a con artist, and a swindler. He was my grandfather's brother on my mother's side. May 12, 1951, on a lonely two-lane dirt road out in the country in Wilcox County, Georgia, he was found shot to death. No murder weapon was found. Nothing of value was taken, not from his car and not from him personally. It looked like retribution.

When the sheriff gave notice to my grandfather of what had happened, he asked Grandfather if he knew of anyone who would want to kill Clark. My grandfather answered, "Half of this county and the next." My grandfather knew his brother. He knew Clark's history, and he also knew he'd slept with a lot of other men's wives. There was probably a list of people who would have wanted to hurt him.

Sometimes your murder victim *is* a criminal. Clark was a lot of things, but he was not violent. He never hurt anybody physically, and none of his crimes deserved the death penalty.

Some of Carl Patton's victims weren't perfect. Some had done some really bad things. But for two of his victims, their only crime was choosing men who weren't good for them. They made bad choices, but they weren't bad people.

Liddie Evans was one of those people. She was a mother of four, and as I was told, she was the life of the party, a good woman, and a loving and devoted mother. Liddie's youngest child, Sylvia, was only six years old when Carl Patton murdered her mother. I asked about her mother. She said, "We were told during the trial that their own daughter, Melissa, had been murdered. I wouldn't wish that pain on anybody."

Liddie's eldest daughter, Renee, who was only sixteen when her momma died and had to take on the role of raising her younger siblings, felt the same way. "I wouldn't wish that hurt on my worst enemy, not even Carl Patton."

Liddie Evans was thirty-one when she was reported missing. At the time, she was living with Joe Cleveland. Although Cleveland had been Carl's best friend since childhood, he was also one of Carl's victims, too.

When people ask me if I think Melissa's murder was payback for Carl's crimes, the implication is maybe a family member of one of Carl's victims got even with him. I wonder if the people asking that are aware they're accusing innocent people of murder. Then the criminologist in me kicks in and I think, Why would a person wait twenty-five years to get even? Why would they not kill Carl? Why Melissa and not Norma? Rather than guessing, I went to the source.

My 361 Vortex method of investigating calls for the full view of this whole tragedy, and Liddie's children were a part of that. I also hoped to dispel the rumors and the questions about whether they, or a member of the other families, might have had something to do with it. I'm a hands-on type person, and this was an issue that needed addressing.

I addressed Liddie's son-in-law, Phillip, first. Phillip is what I call an outside-insider. Although he wasn't born into the family, he's been a member by marriage for many years. Married to Carolyn, he's in this family for better or worse. He said, "We have lived with this tragedy as well."

When I asked him straight up if he had anything to do with Melissa's murder, he gave a low, steady, and strong answer. "Not a thing. In fact, I didn't know that Melissa had been harmed in any way until well after the fact of her dad being put in prison for my wife's mom's murder."

Carolyn shared how they found out about their mother's murder. "Well, if I remember correctly, we got a phone call saying that they had found a body, and we had to go and see who…see about it. They were also showing it on the news about them finding bodies in the Flint River about the time we got the phone call. We went to the hospital, but we didn't get to see Mother's body; they wouldn't allow it because we were so young, I guess."

Her brother Roy continues the story. "I think I was about seventeen when it happened. Renee was fifteen and Carolyn was fourteen and Sylvia was six. Sylvia might have a little bit lesser memories because she was so young."

Although Sylvia was too young to remember, I knew Roy, Renee, and Carolyn would. I asked Renee to tell me about how her mom was the life of the party. "My mom, either she liked you or she didn't like you. But my mom, she would give anything off her back. I don't know of anybody that didn't like our mother. Whatever was going on, she was in, wanting to be part of it, I mean, she was just a good-hearted woman, she was easy-going. She loved her young'uns. She never bothered nobody. She worked and come home and looked after her young'uns and our mother never bothered no one."

Carolyn said, "Momma loved wide-open, didn't she? Meaning, if she loved you, you knew it. She was very truthful. If she liked you, you knew it, and if she didn't like you, you also knew it."

I never knew Liddie, but she sounded like someone I'd like. I love it in a person when you always know where you stand with them.

Hearing them talk about Liddie was powerful. "Y'all lost so much when you lost your momma," I told them. "That's the person that's going to love you the most in this whole world. And for somebody to take her from you, yet you still have care and concern for what happened to Melissa Wolfenbarger."

To me, that set this whole case in such a proper place. By that, I mean no harm should come to anyone. And, if it does, everybody should care about that and want justice for that person.

Sylvia talked so sweetly about Melissa's children. "Like Melissa's kids, I was so young, and I had to grow up knowing that someone did that to my mom, and we didn't know who did it." She hesitated for a moment, gathering her thoughts. "Well, in our case, we knew, but you know there was no justice. And I wouldn't wish that on anybody's children. As far as Carl and Norma, I have no sympathy for them, but I have every amount sympathy in the world for their kids."

Roy didn't mince words when it came to Carl Patton. "The day they sentenced him at the courthouse, that man looked like he didn't have a care in the world, didn't show no compassion or nothing. And, you know what, it was a hard day. I hated it took twenty-five years to lock the man up that killed Mom. And his wife, she helped with everything. And they let her off. I think she should have been locked up along with him because she helped with all of that. I have nightmares to this day about my mother and what he did to her. I remember his face like it was yesterday."

I asked Roy if he always knew Carl murdered his mother. "When I was little, I was staying with Dad, I used to go over to Mom's and Hot Shot [Carl's nickname] would be there. He always carried a gun on his side. Both he and Mom's boyfriend, Joe Cleveland, always carried a gun on their side. Somebody said he was in the Dixie Mafia, said he was a hired killer. If you had the money and wanted somebody dead, Carl Patton would do it. He killed a lot of innocent people. He's getting what he deserved. He should never see daylight or step foot out of that prison again. He should rot in there. Norma should be in there with him."

Renee's been struggling with nightmares her whole life. "I take mental-health meds to this day. The one I take at nighttime—it's for nightmares. And I'm like my brother. I knew that he killed Momma from the get-go. Like my brother said, Carl always had that gun. It had a pearl handle on it. I'll never forget it as long as I live."

According to Carolyn, she and her siblings went to the court dates in DeKalb and Fayette Counties. "We didn't go to the one in Henry County, but we went to the others."

The charges against Carl were a jurisdictional nightmare. The victims were murdered in one county and dumped in the Flint River, but one body floated into Fayette County and another floated into Henry County. To complicate matters even more, Fred Wyatt's body was moved to another county and left in a car on the railroad tracks. Different counties all had victims tied to the same series of murders.

Carolyn recalled the way Carl looked at them in court. "He just looked like he was staring a hole through us. To me, I could just see evil dwelling there. And his wife, when she got on the stand and testified, I remember her illustrating and talking about when the time was right, and this is when he shot her, and she demonstrated how Mother fell over on her couch. And it was like she had no...conscience. She was so insensitive. I mean, she kept a straight face while she was doing all this. She didn't cry, nothing. I just don't understand how people can be so insensitive."

When Carolyn was asked if she felt Norma was afraid of Carl or simply had no remorse, she couldn't answer. "I'm not sure, because I know my mother was afraid of Joe. She was scared of him because he was very possessive and very...you know, like you're going to do what I say or else. So, when momma came up missing, I thought it was the two of them together—Joe and Hot Shot. Joe was abusive to me when nobody was around."

Sylvia was too young to remember a lot about Joe. "I do remember him getting onto me and, you know, standing me in the corner and giving me spankings. But I don't remember a lot of abuse."

Even though Sylvia doesn't remember, her siblings do. Joe Cleveland was abusive toward them and their mother. He also had a criminal record and was known about town as a violent man. I'd heard the same thing about Fred Wyatt, from different people.

Carolyn remembers something Roy said: "My brother said that Carl Patton got what he deserved, but I don't agree with that. He still gets to visit with his family. He gets to see pictures of his grandkids. You know, all the milestones, my sixteenth birthday, when I had children—all the different things, Carl still gets to experience, although behind prison walls, he still gets to experience those things and see his grandkids. And I just don't think it's fair, and I don't think that it's fair for Norma to be walking free."

She had a valid point. There's no question that Carl got to see photographs. He got personal visits. Although from a prison cell, he was able to celebrate milestones—the birthdays, the graduations, the weddings, the babies.

Roy said, "When I went to court, I sat about two or three rows behind Carl Patton and, crazy thoughts ran through my mind. I wish I could just jump across there and just choke him to death for what he did to Mom. Yeah, I wish I could have."

Roy also wishes he could have done more to protect Liddie. "I lived in Alabama with Daddy. My sister lived with Mom in Georgia. I went up there every couple of weekends to see Mom. I wish I could have been… maybe did something and protected her. Because she was a good mom. She was innocent. She wouldn't hurt nobody. It's just rough, you know."

Nightmares aren't exclusive to his sisters. "Yeah, I have nightmares, too. I wake up just in a cold sweat, shaking, and my wife shakes me and tells me to wake up and stuff, and it's just hard."

I told them about Carl's letters, about his remorse, and asked if they were surprised. I shared that he said he didn't realize the pain he'd caused until Melissa's murder. And I asked if they'd mind if I read part of one of the letters to them. I wanted it to be clear it was their choice.

Carolyn was the first to agree, with Roy next. He said, "Yeah, I'd like to hear what he…some of what he had wrote about, anyway."

I began reading Carl's own words. "As I have told you many times, I didn't realize what hurt and harm I done till we lost Melissa. Nothing I can say or do will ever change forty-five years ago. I have asked my family, the families of the victims, and God to forgive me. I know God will, and I understand why the victim's family won't. I will never forgive Chris, so I do understand their hate toward me."

After a moment, Carolyn said, "That surprises me, but I…you know, God doesn't give me the right to hate people. He doesn't give me the right to take life or give it, that's God's job. So as far as forgiving, I don't know that I have, but I don't hate anybody."

Renee's husband Phillip chimed in. "Sheryl, can I play devil's advocate for a second? So having sat in that courtroom watching the lack of remorse in his eyes and wry little grin on the side of his face, as the family suffered, my question would be this: In that letter, is he trying to make himself look good so that someone would help him, or is he trying to play on the sympathy of society, looking forward to a day when he thinks he might see daylight again?"

I told them the feelings and skepticism were valid. "All I can tell y'all is he has stated something similar in numerous letters. Even after the parole board denied his release, he said similar things to me. And, I mean, he wasn't a young kid. It's not that. But he does try to convey that the level of pain and that level of loss, he just never connected it because he had never experienced it."

I gave them a moment to collect their thoughts, then shared my own. "I just wanted y'all to know, at least he's saying it. Because, again, you know, he has no reason to write that to me over and over and over. He's not up for parole again for years. And please understand, Carl Patton and I are not friends. Carl Patton is exactly where he needs to be for the crimes that he committed. There's no doubt about that. The government decided to make a deal with Norma. That's got nothing to do with y'all, either."

It was a the thin edge of the wedge I was traveling down, and I hoped they understood I wasn't making excuses for the man who murdered their mother. "I think when what was done to Melissa came to light, there had to be, whether he had remorse or not, there had to be at least some understanding that what he felt at that moment, he had made somebody else feel the same way. So, I hope he felt that. I hope he now has an understanding of that. And I do hope he's begging everybody for forgiveness. But I agree with you, Phillip, there's no way for me to know whether that's true."

I broached the subject of the Dixie Mafia. "Roy, when I asked him, he said he wasn't a part of the Dixie Mafia. He said that Fred used to like to tell people they were in the Dixie Mafia to get status and to get people to fear them more."

Roy said, "I don't really know. In my heart, I think they were a part of it, you know."

Phillip had an experience that gave him reason to believe that there was a Dixie Mafia connection. "I was just going to say, as an outsider, like you and me were talking when we started, when the investigation of their mom's murder first started twenty-five years later, they started looking into the new DNA and such that was then brought up. I don't know what he was involved in when she was murdered, I wasn't around the family back then. But I do know this: The town that Carolyn and I lived in at the time, I was friends with a lot of police officers and the sheriff in the county where we lived. I found a note on my car and, you know, some rumors were circulating. I got several phone calls at the house that told me to back away and leave it be. I don't know what Carl and Joe were involved in, but twenty-five years later, I received those kinds of messages telling me to back away and leave it alone."

Well, that's a horse of a different color. I wasn't expecting that. I said, "It's scary to think somebody knew your car, where your car was and where your car was parked at a certain time at a certain day, and who you were, as that outside-insider."

I would have never asked if any of Liddie's children had ever been threatened. That hadn't crossed my mind. But now it has.

Phillip asked if he could share his victim-impact statement with me. I told him of course he could. Below is his statement in full.

I asked you if I could write a victim's impact statement from the outside, and I wrote this on February the 22nd after our conversation the day prior. And it says [as read]: I met my wife in high school in Valley, Alabama. Just a strip of a girl, quiet and reserved. She had friends, but not many, as the new kid in school. After high school, she went to college and I joined the military where I would work...where it would work out that we'd come back together in the small town we met. Then a year later, we were married and began our adventure into this new life. Although I knew her mom was deceased, I didn't know all the details until we had been married for a bit. One night I came in to find her crying and very emotional. Then she began to tell me and open up to me about her early teen life and the guy that her mom lived with, and how that he had a best friend named Carl Patton. My wife began to tell me the despicable things that he would say and do and how she always...she was always afraid of Carl, and he always had his gun in this briefcase with him everywhere he went and did [dis]reputable things. The conversation revealed how Liddie went missing around the seventeenth of December. And when the news came, they found her and she had been murdered, found by duck hunters, and her body was floating in the river. It wasn't long, as it worked out, that Joe, Liddie's live-in boyfriend and Carl's best friend, was found on a playground in pretty much the same predicament. I don't know if I can put into words the impact that the loss of her mom has had, but I'm going to try like this. At age fourteen, the transition of age from adolescence to teen, when a young girl needs her mom for guidance and understanding, her mom was snatched away by selfishness and pure meanness. Liddie was not afforded the chance to see her daughter graduate school—high school or college. She was not present at our wedding. She did not get to help planning, her hair, her nails. She didn't get to help pick out the dress. She did not get to dance with her son-in-law, and Liddie was not there for the announcement of our...or the birth of our first child. She was not allowed the opportunity to hold our son and daughter or watch them grow up. Liddie wasn't here to see what a wonderful loving and supporting [unintelligible] and educator that her daughter has grown to be. What a loving grandmother and a daughter she has become, and she wasn't given the chance to meet me or to meet her and build a relationship with her grandchildren and watch them grow up. And these are the things that many...and many other life milestones and events that were simply missed because, in his words, he thought somehow, she wronged him. That shoe fits both ways. For thirty-seven years, I have been celebrating birthdays, Christmas, births, deaths, and watched my wife endure and overcome those empty and lonely days without her mom because of his disrespectful attitude. I have walked through some dark valleys. I've listened to things that turn my stomach that she saw and endured in her teen years at the hand of a selfish man who imposed his will on a child. I see my kids and my grandkids and they ask questions, having to learn about their grandmother, great-grandmother through picture and memories, and I watch the pain in my wife's eyes as she tells them these stories about her, and how the lights...how she lights up when she talks about memories of her mom and the good times that they had. And I know the only ones, no, I don't harbor feelings. I don't harbor feeling. I promise. No, it does break my heart. It hurts my feelings. And, yes, would I or

> do I wish this pain on nobody, no. What—for twenty-five years of not knowing, not knowing why, not knowing how, not knowing who, and now that we do know, and this pain has befallen him, I have to ask myself this. Does he really have remorse? Does he actually think that one of us would have exacted revenge, not knowing where he was, who he was, or that he even had a daughter? And I would ask this question: For twenty-five years, he left Liddie Evans's family wondering the same thing that he's wondering now. And the question would be this: Can you help him find justice for his daughter so that maybe his mind will rest and the words that he wrote to you would be true in his life. I pray for the man every day, but I'm a victim of his abuse and his selfishness and that's…I guess that's all I'm going to say.

After a moment, I said, "I always preach this ripple effect, and you're part of that ripple effect, and your children and your grandchildren. They're in the ripple effect that I talk about. Carl Patton has no idea how many people he's hurt. How many teachers, fellow students, how many neighbors, how many people from different congregations, no telling how many good friends of all of these people."

Carolyn said, "I don't know where to start. It's not been easy. I'm currently seeing a therapist because of all this stuff that has built up in my life. I do hope they find justice for his daughter. I know what it's like to lose a child, and I wouldn't wish that on anybody. But, at the same time, God doesn't give us the right to take life. He had no right. No matter what people do, two wrongs don't make a right. Even if she had wronged him, it doesn't make a right because God is the giver and taker of life, not man. I have no hard feelings either because God would not allow me to harbor hard feelings against this person. I'm like my husband, I pray because God gives everybody a soul, and we all are going to go to heaven or hell one day. As a follower of Christ, I have to pray for his soul. You know, it doesn't make the hurt go away. It doesn't make the pain go away. Only God is helping me with this pain. He's helping me take one day at a time and see—and helping me overcome. And, you know, God says we're overcomers by his Word, so that's all I can rely on. And I just pray they find the justice, and I pray that he truly, truly, truly understands the pain that we've endured all these years, and all the things he stripped out of my life in talking my mother."

I told them what Carolyn had said was perfectly stated. I then asked Renee if she wanted to add anything. She said, "Yes, ma'am. I just want to say that what my sister said is true. There's nothing that can take away the pain or the hurt. And it seems like the older I get—and I know this is going to sound weird, but the older I get, the more I need my mom. I mean, I'll always need her, but it seems the older I get the more I need her, and she's not there for me to take her advice. And the sad thing about it to me is, her grandchildren that she's missed seeing and growing up and it's just…I hope, like my sister, I do not…you know, I don't wish the hate, the pain or hurt on anyone and I just hope that one day, that he just really, truly does understand the hurt and the pain he's caused. And I want to thank you for having this so we can all tell our story, say what we had to say. And there's just one more thing I want to say. I just want people to know that my mom—our mother—was the best, good-hearted, and hardworking woman that you'd ever meet."

Roy took his turn slow and deliberate. "Well, like I say, we've said, Mom's never seen my daughter, my grandkids. She's missed all of the birthdays, Christmas and stuff. I live with this every day. I miss my mom every day. Mom was good to me. And she would have been a wonderful grandmother. My daughter and grandkids don't know what they are missing, because Mom would have been…she would have done anything for them. And it's just been hard. And the justice system, I think they failed us. I think they should have given Carl Patton a death penalty, and I think they should have given his wife life without parole. Oh, I hate that about his daughter, you know. I wouldn't wish that on nobody to lose their kid, but, for Carl Patton, I will never forgive the man. I don't like the man, and

I'll never forgive him until the day that I die. And we thank you for having us on your podcast, but I've been wanting to get this off my chest for a while, and I thank you for that."

Sylvia finished by saying, "And I just want to say, first of all, I don't know if they listen, but thank you to Bruce Jordan and Trace Farr for coming down after twenty-five years. I know it takes a community and police officers. But they are the two that were there for us and Bruce's inclination to open the case back up. So, I want to say thanks to them if they are listening. But, you know, I was thirty-one years old during the trial, the same age that Mom was when she passed. And, at the time, I already had two kids that she never got to see. And that's all I could think about during the trial. You know, you deprived me and deprived my two sons, and Momma. If she were here, would have her first great-great grandchild this May. She missed all of that. I don't know if I could forgive him but, like my sister, I don't hate anyone. But I'll never forgive him, and we can't forget. We remember every birthday, every holiday, all our kids' birthday, because she's not there."

Before closing, I said, "I believe Liddie is a part of each one of her children in all that y'all have done with all of your children and grandchildren; the children that y'all touched in the neighborhood; school, churches, and neighborhoods. All of you have done remarkable things for other people, and that is because of her. There's no doubt. So if Liddie Evans were alive and well right now, she'd be spreading love and joy. Ain't no question 'bout it. And all of her children—this is the most important thing to me and I know would be important to her—y'all are all together. I believe in family, honey, and y'all are tight and it's wonderful and there's a lot of tears today. But y'all are in the same house right now, and that's a powerful thing to me."

I ended the show by adding, "Dr. Eric Hickey said, and I quote, 'Every person can make a difference and every person should try.' End quote. Stephanie Roper, twenty-two, wrote this in her diary two days before she was raped and murdered. And Dr. Hickey wrote to me on September 28, 2007, and simply said, 'Do these cold cases.' Well, as I speak to the children of Liddie Evans, they are making a difference. They are nurses. They are teachers. They are parents. They are grandparents. They are good, nonviolent, loving and caring citizens, and I appreciate each one of them talking with me."

Chapter 16

ZONE 7

IN MY CAREER, I HAVE been lucky. Don't misunderstand, I have worked hard, gained an education, and had superior training, but I have been extremely lucky, too. One of the most important and hand-of-God, career-changing events happened organically and without preparation.

In 1992, I was assigned to the major case division at the Crime Commission. It was about 2:45 a.m., and we were at an active crime scene, tons of police everywhere, detectives huddled together, neighbors standing around outside, and all of a sudden this sports car comes barreling toward the yellow tape sliding in sideways and a little bitty person pops out yelling, "Whata y'all have, where we at, how I can help!"

I said out loud to our group, "What is that?"

Jim Burch with the Georgia Bureau of Investigation said, "That's Nancy Grace with the DA's office." I knew two things in that moment: Our case just got better, and Nancy Grace and I were going to be friends!

We did become friends and are still close today. I can tell you that meeting Nancy changed not just my career but my life. I wouldn't have the career I have today without her. Her influence, her unwavering support, and her unfailing friendship.

Nancy loves to tell people "we worked in the trenches" together "in the city of Atlanta." We, in fact, worked some of the most violent, dangerous, and horrifying streets and cases together. We worked in the cut, in the bluff, and in the gutter often. We searched for witnesses, suspects, and victims at all hours of the day and night. We worked weekends, overtime, and holidays.

Nancy Grace is the best victim advocate I've ever seen in action. She was the first ADA that I ever saw come out to a crime scene in the middle of the night. I rarely saw one at a scene during the day, much less in the dark. Our cases were personal to us. They still are. Don't be fooled by Nancy being on TV. These are cases to her. Cases that she is "working." Working in her way, methodical and deliberate. Her mind is always running, searching, plotting, planning, and investigating.

Nancy was a crime victim. She used her tragedy to serve others. To ensure that justice would be served each and every time someone was harmed at the hands of a criminal. I have witnessed her devotion time and time again. I remember once at her apartment she had several case files spread across her bed. She prayed over each and every file. She prayed for the victims, their families, the police, the detectives, and her office to do the right thing by the victim.

This friendship with Nancy is how *Zone 7* came to be. When we were working the streets with police, there were no cell phones yet, no pagers, so we had to get creative when planning after-shift social gatherings.

There were two different events—one we called Choir Practice and the other, Zone 7. Choir Practice would be a group that gathered after a shift to talk about the events we experienced that day or night. Kind of an informal debriefing that included drinking. Anyone and everyone who wanted to come could stop by and enjoy the camaraderie and great storytelling. This event normally took place in the police parking lot or at a secure location.

Every so often we needed more than Choir Practice. We needed our inner circle. The trusted, battle-tested, fiercely supportive, ride-or-die folks. We needed someone to tell us the truth, help us understand the job, the case, or the boss. The folks who had your best interests at all times. They protect you, support you, teach you, and have your 6.

Atlanta has six police zones. So when we needed a meetup with our circle, we would call out over the radio to 59 (meet) at Zone 7 at 1900

(7:00 p.m.). Seven at seven was easy to remember and easy to get to. For my circle, Zone 7 was Manuel's Tavern.

Manuel's is drenched in local history. The walls are covered with political, police, and Atlanta memorabilia. Back in the day we would arrive, Manuel would be sitting in his booth ready to greet us, have a table waiting for us where we could talk openly and privately. The drinks would come quickly but the food slow enough to give us time to settle into our much-needed fellowship.

The deep mahogany wooden bar hung over us like a physical roll call of the crimes, prosecutors, cops, and detectives that came before us. Between paintings and police badges, news articles and photographs, are other artifacts that only insiders would see or know their importance. I have one relic on that bar.

It was in this bar, with these people among our things that Nancy Grace gave me some wisdom that I have carried every day of my career. We had been driving around the bluff looking for a witness to a murder. Our CIs had told us a few places to try to locate her. Every flophouse, underpass, and street corner that turned up a bust, Nancy would talk to others at the location asking if they might know where to find "Angel" (not her real name). The officer with us was getting frustrated and wanted to stop this "pointless search." He didn't believe we were ever going to find her.

If you know Nancy Grace this only served to fuel her fire. I thought, *If this boy don't stop complaining, she'll drive us to Chattanooga searching for Angel.* After our search that night ended, we met with several friends at Manuel's for a Zone 7 dinner. Nancy was regaling everyone about our efforts, and I added that we had dealt with some characters on our quest. Nancy smiled and turned to me and said, "Swans don't swim in a sewer."

It hit me dead in my twenty-something-year-old face. Of course we had spoken to hookers, pimps, the homeless, drug addicts, and petty criminals looking for Angel, because they were who would know where she was hiding out. Preachers, nurses, teachers, and Fortune 500 folks would have no clue. Nancy has given me a surplus of great advice over the years, but I have built an investigative body of work off of this colorful, quick-witted statement. During the Olympic Park bombing, we interviewed as many sex workers we could find in order to see who was in town. Did anyone brag about this crime, make them pretend to be a victim, make them hold a bomb? During the investigation into the Moore's Ford Bridge lynching, I sought the expertise of a former Wizard of the KKK. Who else would know if these murders were a Klan hit? During the Tupac Shakur investigation, I befriended Frank Cullotta, ex-Mafia hit man. And now, during the investigation into the gruesome murder of Melissa Wolfenbarger, I sought out a killer to seek intel on her killer.

It was a no-brainer. After all these years, of course I would include talking with Melissa's father. I would talk with the father of any other victim, but this case was different because of her father's background. I knew that including him might just draw the killer out and cause him to slip up, maybe talk more.

Everyone was working on Melissa's case, and Carl sat trapped in a cell. He couldn't do what he'd like to do to help. I told him once during our first call that he and I were working this case together. He seemed to like that and felt empowered to contribute. I explained that between our letters, Norma's passing information to him on her Saturday visits once a month, and our secret calls when he could finagle the use of a cell phone, he was my partner. I jokingly told him he most likely was the best partner because he couldn't dictate when and where my day started, what I had for lunch, who drove the car, or who wrote the report. In fact, it took two weeks to hear back from him if he didn't like what I was doing. By that time, it was over and done. No need to argue.

Carl laughed and said, "You better not put that in the book. Leslie won't like that, and aren't you afraid of her?"

Leslie had been my partner during the 1996 Olympics, 911 Response Team, Cobb DA's office and Juvenile Court to name a few, and best friend. I responded, "Carl you've killed five people, and I'm more afraid of Leslie." He was still laughing as we hung up the phone.

I have on occasion received criticism for seeking out these "specialists." Carl Patton was not the first criminal I had worked with, nor will he be the last. I have worked with and sought intelligence from Johnny Lee Clary, the ex-Imperial Wizard for the KKK; Mafia hit man Frank Cullotta; David Berkowitz, aka the Son of Sam; and numerous sex workers and rogue cops, just to name a few.

I know that it's imperative to go to the source. Talk with someone who has information and knowledge that you don't. I love it when people ask things like, "The Klan? How did you get in touch with them?" They're expecting some police operation with covert actions involving clandestine meetings. I love the look on their face when I say, "The KKK has an 800 number—I just called them!"

Go to the source. It will never fail you.

Chapter 17

ROADBLOCKS, OBSTACLES, AND WALLS

FAMILIES OF MURDER VICTIMS, ESPECIALLY in cold cases, often have outside issues, political events, or other entanglements that halt, alter, or postpone justice for their loved one. Melissa's case was certainly no different.

Melissa's case got so little attention that her probation officer took out warrants for failure to show up for her scheduled meeting. They didn't know she was missing. I guess Christopher ignored the mail and phone calls. If he believed she left, he allowed a warrant to be issued for her arrest. If this is true, he was not going to let her just leave him. He was going to make sure she went back to jail. One would have to ask is he just a POS or her killer.

All too often the detective assigned to a case will retire, transfer, or get promoted away from the case. Melissa's family had already lost their original detective to retirement and were set to lose the DA investigator to a transfer. I wanted to be sure that Melissa's case was on the radar of the incoming district attorney, Fani Willis.

I called her and set up a meeting between the two of us prior to her taking office. I wanted to highlight several cold cases I knew could be solved with the right team and funding. The funding we were going to take care of, but I needed a prosecutor willing to champion these cases. On October 30, 2020, at approximately 10:00 a.m., I walked into DA-elect Willis's office off of Piedmont. She was alone in the house that had been turned into headquarters for her campaign. She opened the door with a bright, warm smile.

After a few pleasantries I said, "I'm not here for a job, I got a job! And I don't need any money!"

She laughed and said, "Have a seat."

We talked for over an hour as I told her about five cases in detail and without stopping. I knew the longer I talked the better the chances of getting these cases moved forward to solve. She listened, took notes, and asked questions.

When I was done with my summation, she looked at me, smiled, and said, "I've already picked the perfect person to head up my Cold Case Task Force. Her name is Adriane Love. She is smart and won't back down. We want you on the task force. The first week we are in office she'll come meet with you."

True to her word, the first week they took office Adriane Love was sitting in *my* office. She was smart, fierce, and determined. She took notes, asked questions, and then went to work. We solved two cases from my list right off the bat!

Melissa's was next on the list. ADA Love was bought in again, dialed in and laser focused. Working these cases, she had met with me numerous times, walked the scenes, met with the families and other experts, and then the twisted hand of criminal justice stepped in. She was pulled from the Cold Case Task Force and put on the RICO trial of the YSL Gang and the rapper Young Thug. We lost one of the best ADAs we'd ever had on cold cases.

The Patton family felt this loss. They felt ADA Love was connected and understood Melissa. They believed that she didn't hold Carl's past over them. She only wanted justice for Melissa. Carl was paying his debt. Now Melissa's killer needed to pay his.

Although we'd lost Adriane, Investigator Richard Stein was still on board, and that made the transition to a new ADA easier for Norma and Tina. Richard was a veteran investigator who wanted badly to reinterview Christopher. He wanted him in a room one-on-one. He had walked the scene with us along with ADA Love. He had met the family and the other experts. He knew this case was solvable and wanted to have a hand in it.

Then, Richard was transferred out of Cold Case. The family felt like Melissa was losing ground. They saw less and less action and received less and less feedback from detectives and the DA's office. I tried to be positive and upbeat, reminding them we were closer than ever before to seeing an arrest made. But weeks turned into months. And months turned into years.

~

It was late and my phone rang. I heard a loud, raspy voice holler, "Fucking Trump. Are you kidding me?"

I didn't need caller ID. I knew it was Tina Patton, Melissa's sister.

I said, "I know, I know. It's a slight setback, but it's not over. We just have to be patient a little longer."

Tina was justifiably upset because once again Melissa's case was taking a back seat to a new issue. DA Fani Willis had indicted a former president of the United States, and with that on her plate there was no way Melissa's case was going to a grand jury. As the world watched Donald Trump turn himself into the Fulton County Sheriff's Office for his famous mug shot, all I could think about was all the families who now had to wait longer for justice. All the accused who now had to wait longer for their day in court to be exonerated. It was a pitiful waste of time and money that was never going to trial—never. This wouldn't be the last or most ridiculous reason Melissa's case was stalled from going to a grand jury.

DA Willis was accused of having an affair with the special prosecutor she hired to prosecute Donald Trump. She was now having to testify about her relationship, money dealings, and ethics related to her office. Melissa once again was pushed to the back while this played out.

Fani Willis has never been anything but nice to me. She was true to her word. We did some great work together. But I'm reminded of the lesson I learned from famed GBI Agent Jim Burch when he headed up

Operation Weed and Seed with the US Department of Justice that I was lucky enough to serve on: "Never give the impression of impropriety." During Operation Weed and Seed, we held an event for children in the most violent communities in Atlanta's infamous Zone 3. There was a dinner hosted by the heavyweight champion of the world, Evander Holyfield. Two rookie officers at the restaurant ordered frozen drinks without alcohol. These drinks came in fancy cocktail glasses with decorative fruit and a colorful paper umbrella. Jim immediately dismissed both from the operation that night. From a distance, and to the children, these officers appeared as if they were not only drinking alcohol, they were doing so in uniform and on duty.

In Fani's case, no matter the outcome, there was the appearance of an affair that she benefitted from with trips and money. That should have never happened. Fani should have had at least one true friend to stop her from traveling and exchanging money with someone under her employment. It's a bad look. And it is a sad day when such a promising career is reduced to memes. But above all else, these national headlines affect the very victims in these jurisdictions, by pushing victims like Melissa right out of the headlines and off everyone's radar.

Chapter 18

THE MONIKER MAKES THE KILLER

IN THE FIRST LETTER I received from Carl, he referred to Melissa in the present tense. He said his daughter was stolen from her two children and family that *loves* her very much. I remember reading that word over and over again. Carl wasn't in denial; he knew Melissa was dead. But the love her family felt for her wasn't. It was still active and ever present.

Carl stated in his letter that he had lost confidence in the Atlanta Police Department. He said that Bruce Jordan kept him from getting answers, Fulton County had stopped Bruce from getting answers, and he wanted to ask me if I was going to let anyone stop me.

The Department of Corrections tried to. I made requests to have time with Carl, to interview him face-to-face. The requests were denied. Karyn Greer made the same requests, and they, too, were denied. So we resorted to handwritten letters with Carl through mail and the occasional secret phone call. Not the most efficient way to interview someone, but it was all we had.

The irony of the denials wasn't lost on me. I've never been one to slam my hands on my hips and scream foul, but I came close. There were certainly times I wanted to.

Other killers—famous notorious killers—were allowed visits, calls, and interviews, but Carl was denied the opportunity to meet with experts to help solve his daughter's case.

Convicted serial killer Wayne Williams has phone privileges. Wayne Williams has media privileges. There are numerous TV interviews you can look up on the internet. Mostly he talks about his innocence. I personally know two people who speak with him weekly and sometimes daily. A child killer who has never had the decency to admit what he did. He has never sent the families a message of sorrow and regret. Carl had done both. But Carl couldn't talk to me or be interviewed by Karyn Greer to shed light on his daughter's case.

One of the most famous and violent killers in Georgia history, Carl Isaacs, was interviewed from prison. As a matter of fact, the DOC allowed the media to talk to him from death row. Carl Isaacs, in my opinion, is one of the most diabolical killers in Georgia history. He once stated, "As far as pulling that trigger and killing them people, I believe it would have happened again." His hellish words should have prevented that interview. Neither of these convicted killers were being interviewed to help another person. Neither offered an apology or remorse. Only self-serving duplicity.

It's not like the Department of Corrections stops crimes from being committed by inmates on the inside. Arthur Lee Cofield managed to scam a billionaire out of $11 million from his Charles Schwab account. That crime was pulled off while Cofield was serving a fourteen-year sentence for bank robbery. From inside the prison, he turned the money into gold coins and then used a portion to buy a $4.4 million mansion in Buckhead.

But Carl Patton couldn't call me about the murder of his child.

Carl Patton was a killer. Carl Patton admitted that several times in open court. Carl Patton was punished for his crimes. But he was severely wronged by not being allowed access to experts and media that were trying to solve a cold case. The Georgia Department of Corrections would rather have had a killer go free than allow Carl to meet with me. Insanity.

Carl Patton photo taken in 1976.

The first photo I ever saw of Melissa Wolfenbarger.

Melissa Wolfenbarger's ninth grade picture.

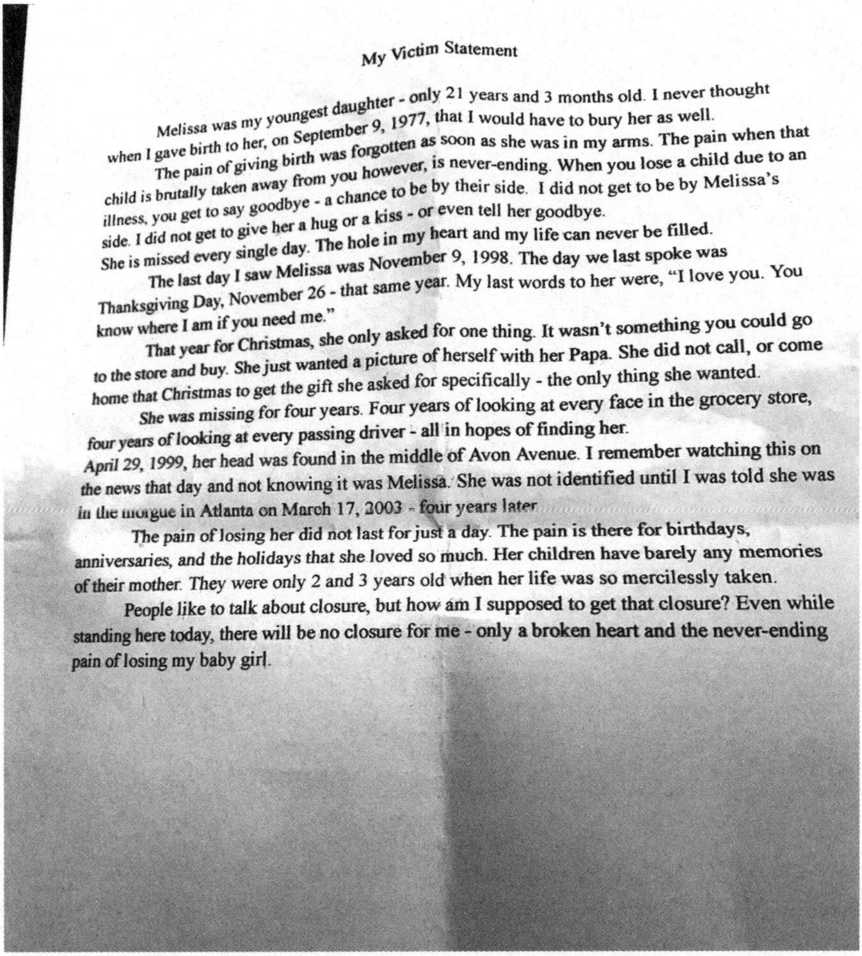

My Victim Statement

Melissa was my youngest daughter - only 21 years and 3 months old. I never thought when I gave birth to her, on September 9, 1977, that I would have to bury her as well.

The pain of giving birth was forgotten as soon as she was in my arms. The pain when that child is brutally taken away from you however, is never-ending. When you lose a child due to an illness, you get to say goodbye - a chance to be by their side. I did not get to be by Melissa's side. I did not get to give her a hug or a kiss - or even tell her goodbye. She is missed every single day. The hole in my heart and my life can never be filled.

The last day I saw Melissa was November 9, 1998. The day we last spoke was Thanksgiving Day, November 26 - that same year. My last words to her were, "I love you. You know where I am if you need me."

That year for Christmas, she only asked for one thing. It wasn't something you could go to the store and buy. She just wanted a picture of herself with her Papa. She did not call, or come home that Christmas to get the gift she asked for specifically - the only thing she wanted.

She was missing for four years. Four years of looking at every face in the grocery store, four years of looking at every passing driver - all in hopes of finding her. April 29, 1999, her head was found in the middle of Avon Avenue. I remember watching this on the news that day and not knowing it was Melissa. She was not identified until I was told she was in the morgue in Atlanta on March 17, 2003 - four years later.

The pain of losing her did not last for just a day. The pain is there for birthdays, anniversaries, and the holidays that she loved so much. Her children have barely any memories of their mother. They were only 2 and 3 years old when her life was so mercilessly taken.

People like to talk about closure, but how am I supposed to get that closure? Even while standing here today, there will be no closure for me - only a broken heart and the never-ending pain of losing my baby girl.

Norma Patton's victim impact statement that she never got to read.

Norma Patton the first night we met.

Me and Tina Patton at the scene of Melissa's body disposal sight.

The manhole cover where Melissa's skull was found in front of Action Glass.

Fani Willis and me at DA Fanni Willis's swearing in ceremony.

Deputy Shepard, Nancy Grace, Norma Patton, and me at the dinner celebrating an arrest in Melissa's case.

Chapter 19

POT LIKKER

MARY MAC'S TEA ROOM IS an Atlanta icon. Nancy Grace and I would take our mothers there the weeks we had money. This was Zone 7 adjacent. My husband, Walt, and I made our way down the sidewalk off Piedmont Avenue. We walked under the historic old red sign with the classic white letters pointing the way inside. The sign has rested on this modest one-story building with the small window boxes full of flowers since 1945. The kitchen is like your grandma's front porch. They shuck bushels of corn and snap peas all by hand. In the early mornings, driving past on our way to the courthouse, the smell of baking fresh breads and desserts wafted outside like a scented reminder to come back for lunch or supper. They'll have the Georgia "table wine" (sweet tea) or the Atlanta champagne (Coca-Cola) waiting for you.

Many major cases have been discussed at Mary Mac's over fried chicken, fried okra, and fried green tomatoes. Margaret Lupo, the late owner, used to greet us personally. She would often point out some of the famous guests who have dined in her beloved Tea Room. Their photographs and autographs hung proudly in every single room.

In the old days, Nancy Grace and I would take our mothers there to talk about South Georgia, cases, or if Nancy should run for DA or head to New York City for a cable TV gig. You were guaranteed to see political powerhouses, famed defense attorneys or prosecutors, singers or actors. We once took our mothers, and that dinner was a special treat. I remember Joe Drolet, an old school prosecutor, stopped by the table after a day at the state capital, and that was a moment to behold. His brilliance and Nancy's storytelling made for an impressive meal. It's a tradition to take our town guests to Mary Mac's and let them experience firsthand our Southern traditions in the kitchen. My favorite is ordering first-timers a cup of pot likker and cornbread!

Walt and I took Norma Patton and a friend, Jeanne Ayotte, to Mary Mac's to talk about the next steps in Melissa's case. Neither Norma or Jeanne had ever been to Mary Mac's, nor had they ever experienced pot likker. Well, they weren't gonna be able to say that in the morning!

Jeanne Ayotte is a smart, adventurous, generous human being. She has funded testing on cold cases, paying for experts to get the training needed at the scene of the crime. She wants no credit or fanfare for doing so; she only wants to help. She came to Atlanta because she won an auction to work a cold case with me, and we selected Melissa's case. Jeanne served our country in the US Coast Guard and has since devoted herself to paralegal work and her family. Her insight and vast knowledge of many different areas helped give this case an additional viewpoint from a clear perspective.

Despite the atmosphere and the down home food, this was a working dinner. We needed to outline what we had and where the case stood. I wanted to bring everyone up to speed on my conversations with Carl and what we believed was needed to get justice for Melissa. During his interview with *Dateline*, Sergeant Layton said, "When Christopher Wolfenbarger was questioned by police, he told them Melissa had left on her own. He then refused to cooperate with the investigation." The sergeant added, "Wolfenbarger has an extensive criminal history with a history of family violence, and witnesses stated during the investigation that he had been abusive to Melissa."

When interviewed, Christopher made several statements to *Dateline* that I found curious. One that leaped out at me was when he said, "Yeah, I have a criminal history. But I'm not a murderer." That is not a denial. He didn't say, "I did not kill Melissa."

He went on to say that Melissa's disappearance at the end of 1998 "wasn't anything out of the ordinary."

That raised my eyebrow, too. Your young wife up and leaves with no car, no money, no phone, no clothes, and without her children and that was not out of the ordinary? She had never gone missing before. She had never gone away without her sister and parents knowing where she was. Hell, even when she left Chris for a short time, *he* knew where she was. Her disappearance was anything *but* ordinary.

"We're not talking about one day she was there and the next she was not," Wolfenbarger said to *Dateline*. "I just figured she'd come back when she was able to."

When she was able to? Did he know something others didn't? Did he know she *wasn't* able to come back?

Christopher explained that Melissa took on multiple shifts at the Waffle House to make extra money and said she'd stay at a hotel instead of commuting home. He added that she also had been creating fake IDs and Social Security cards with the goal of their family moving away and starting a new life in California. He just threw her under the bus again. Like himself, he was saying, she had her criminal ways.

"I'm not denying I have criminal history," he said. "We were, you know, like Bonnie and Clyde, just small-time criminals, but we didn't do anything bad, bad. We were just trying to build a better life…in California. California was the dream."

But how did she get to California? She had no money. No car. No means to travel three thousand miles. That part of his story certainly didn't add up.

Once the truth came out that Melissa had been murdered, her "loving husband" never demanded police action. He never went on TV demanding justice. He was never fearful the killer would come and harm him or the children. Why not? Was it because he knew who the killer was and that he was in zero danger? This dinner at Mary Mac's gave us additional questions and helped us see where the case was lacking and where it was strong. I got to talk to Carl again.

Chapter 20

5 PERCENT OF THE TIME

I WAS HONORED TO BE a part of the DA's Office Cold Case Task Force. Assistant District Attorney Adriane Love invited me to a meeting at the Roswell Police Department. She was excited to get this unit rolling, and I could hear the excitement in her voice. As I walked into the room with Adriane, the snack table caught my eye.

The oldest trick in the book for getting cops to show up for a meeting—feed them. I laughed to myself thinking of all the trainings, meetings, and events where I had to first promise food before anyone even asked what the training, meeting, or event was about.

The room was full of accomplished detectives, higher-ups, and representatives from the Fulton County DA's office. The DA's office sent an investigator and two additional ADAs. At this first meeting, Adriane laid out her wish list for attacking these unsolved cases.

Adriane was clear we needed no egos. What we did need were solid leads and a plan of action for these cases. She emphasized that this task force was a team, so any one person's success would be everyone's success. I knew she'd get two out of three of those wants.

The ego part was going to be difficult. Ego is a funny thing in Homicide. I believe some folks are drawn to it because of past pain, some for the need to help, and others for the heroics. I can usually determine someone's motive for wanting to work homicides fairly quickly and without a doubt why they want to work cold cases. Ego is an important aspect of any job in criminal justice, and it's really not a bad thing. You have to *believe* you can hunt down a killer in order to do it. However, the ego needs to be kept in check to work as a team and either share credit or give it all away. I have said many times I could care less who gets the credit if that means a killer is off the streets. Unfortunately, everyone doesn't share that sentiment.

Once Adriane was taken off Melissa's case for the RICO case on YSL and Young Thug, a new head of the task force stepped in to take the lead. That kind of shake-up gives opportunists a window to exert their authority or expertise. The change can determine the true leaders from the self-important opportunists. All the good work, effort, and time you've put into a case can come to a grinding stop if a true leader doesn't take the reins.

I have a rule about team meetings. If you are not running the meeting, the invited expert, or the lead outlining a case, you should talk no more than 5 percent of the time. If you are not the above-listed folks, no one came to the meeting to hear you. You are not adding to the meeting. You in fact are wasting everyone's time with your thoughts, unsolicited advice, and opinions. When everyone in the room is accomplished, educated, trained, and experienced, you should not be a self-appointed co-chair. My husband, Walt, runs a department for the Home Depot headquarters. He holds "stand up" meetings where everyone stands the whole time. This cuts down unnecessary chatter that only stalls the work at hand.

I remember one Cold Case Task Force meeting where a detective "ran" the meeting. His cases, his ideas, his thoughts, his opinions. It was exhausting, and very little got done on the cases that day. Including Melissa's.

Chapter 21

CONTRABAND

MY CELL PHONE RANG ON February 28, 2022, showing a 229 area code. I knew that was South Georgia. Unlike a lot of folks in my business, I answer calls from numbers I don't have locked in my phone.

When I answered, I heard a low, raspy voice on the other end of the line. "Ms. Sheryl, it's Carl Patton."

Now, I knew Carl didn't have access legally to a phone, so I knew this must be important. He thanked me for helping Norma and wanted to get my honest opinion whether an arrest would ever be made for the murder of Melissa.

I wanted to tell him to not get discouraged. We added a witness, a geo profile, statement analysis, and located evidence. I am a glass half full person and life my friend Joshua Schiffer says, "You can refill that glass. I have tried to show my child Huck and Caroline big picture everything. If its not going to matter in a year don't spend one minute worrying about it." Carl had to see all the progess we had made; he had made.

I wondered if Carl and Norma cheered from the stands when Melissa performed with the baton team. It wasn't important now. What was important was reassuring Carl that despite what it looked like from where he sat, we were making progress in Melissa's case.

Carl and I had first started communicating in March of 2021 through letters. That exchange of information was like watching two turtles racing toward a finish line. Norma visited with Carl once a week and relayed the questions and information about the investigation between me and Carl. Imagine the frustration you'd feel if you had a burning question but knew it'd be a week before you got an answer. The timetable was torture!

Now imagine you're the parent of a murdered child and you want answers, you want justice. You want to pick up the phone and call the detective in charge and ask where they were with the investigation. If you got their voicemail, you might even pay them a visit at their office and ask about new leads. Suppose you had information you knew would be helpful, but despite all the new-fangled technology we have at our disposable to communicate with, you were reduced to handwriting letters and waiting for the reply, and making notes for the next weekly visit.

Welcome to our world.

While in prison, Carl had been a model inmate. He had successfully completed education courses and stayed out of trouble. But he was a desperate man trying to help find justice for his child. He had to rely on others. In prison for the murder of five people, he couldn't avenge his baby girl's gruesome death even if he'd wanted to. Tina Mae told me one time her dad would often tell her, "If you ever need me, you know where I am." I took that to mean Carl Patton could help her no matter where he was—inside or out. The cell phones, no non-family visitors, and Tina's "just say the word if you need me" statement…I was back to thinking Carl had connections to outside criminal elements. He'd been very clear he wasn't part of the Dixie Mafia, but sometimes he sure moved that way.

When he called me that day, I knew he was taking a chance. I didn't want to know where he got the phone. He asked me what my plan was. "How are you going to get answers that others haven't?"

I told him I believed if we could locate the trash bags and do forensic testing, there was a chance, slim, but a chance, that inside the tied knots there could be the killer's DNA. I explained that I had already reached out to my friend and forensics expert, Francine Bardole. She knew the case and was the most capable person I knew to test the knots.

Francine invented the Bardole Method of extracting DNA from spent shell casings. Most experts believed it was impossible due to the fire and heat when the projectile was expelled. Francine proved even the experts wrong and has been remarkably successful in collecting DNA off spent casings. I had every confidence that if there was DNA from the killer on the trash bags, she would find it.

Assistant Chief Investigator Richard Stein was phenomenal in locating the evidence and getting it sent to Francine. Richard and Adriane again had done everything they said they were going to do from the start. Even though she was removed from the case, she was still head of the Cold Case Unit.

Male DNA was located! I may have held my breath while waiting for the results.

On March 31, 2023, the results came back. Christopher Wolfenbarger was excluded.

There were plenty of killers in prison who were convicted without DNA evidence. Law enforcement back in the days before DNA had to put together a murder case based on eyewitnesses, fingerprints, bogus alibis, and circumstantial evidence. Melissa's case wasn't that different.

We had to go street level. But that's where I like it! Time to hunt down other witnesses: neighbors, coworkers, probation officers, and detectives. We had to back up and go old school. Statements, pre- and post-behavior, criminal history, and other factors had to be looked at again in this case. It was boots on the ground time.

We also needed to go back to the preacher Christopher Wolfenbarger all but confessed to. The man was Christopher's mother's preacher who had come forward with information. We needed to take a seat on a pew.

We were able to track down and call a detective from another jurisdiction who had investigated a domestic violence case against Chris. I'll never forget—the detective said she told Melissa, "If you don't get away from him for good, he's gonna kill you."

That statement gave credence to the violence Melissa suffered at the hands of her husband. A trained law enforcement officer who had worked family violence cases for years saw the red flags. She warned Melissa about the dangers of staying in the relationship. She warned her about the risks involved in a volatile relationship and how quickly things can escalate out of control. Even escalating to murder. Adriane Love and Richard Stein again went to great lengths in locating and speaking with this retired detective. They were steadily putting a case together.

Carl called me numerous times over the years. The calls were few and far between, and they always had an urgency about them. He often needed reassurance that the DA's office hadn't given up. He told me he didn't understand all the delays and stalls in the investigation. I reminded him we were closer than we had ever been. Since he and I first talked we had located evidence and gotten it tested in a private lab, we located an additional witness, we visited the scene and searched for more remains and the saw. We had the DA buy in, and ADA buy in, and a lead DA's investigator buy in. We presented Melissa's case to a national audience—twice. We were able to consult numerous experts across the US, and each and every one believed her husband was responsible for her murder. We were instrumental in getting the Atlanta Police Department to reinterview Chris, interview his mother and sister, and talk again to the preacher.

If not for *Dateline* covering Melissa's case, law enforcement would not have new additional statements from Christopher. The new interview from the coverage would give law enforcement another statement from Christopher to cross-check against past statements. I reached out to the DA's office and offered the services of Peter Hyatt, an expert in statement analysis. The offer was to have Peter analyze all statements made by Chris and pull out any deception that might exist. He would then formulate questions to ask and in what order for Christopher's next police interview. I also believed Peter could help develop the questions for Christopher's mother and sister.

Once Adriane Love was transferred, everything stopped. The next steps were once again pushed just beyond our reach.

Carl and I often talked about the importance of getting different experts to look at this case. The more experts we had offering their expertise, the better. We had K9s, crime mapping, statement analysis, DNA, knots, domestic violence, media, and scene search experts in the bag. We needed all the ammo we could gather to present to the prosecutor for a full view of the potential leverage this case had.

At one stage of my law enforcement career, I worked eight years for the Fulton County Sheriff's Office in the infamous Rice Street jail. It was constant noise. Once you entered the front and the doors slammed behind you, it was a different world. A world most people don't know anything about.

You can watch all the TV shows about jail and prison you want, but there's a few key basics left out. One, watching TV is safe. No one is going to fight you, stab you, rape you, or kill you. You won't be taken hostage and held by criminals for a long period of time. Two, you just can't appreciate the stench. Hundreds of men and women sweating, bleeding, and not bathing. It is a smell like no other and undeniable. A near-nauseating concoction of bodily fluids, filth, and decay. Three, the never-ending noise. The sounds compete against one another to see which can be the loudest until they fuse together into one giant cacophony. Your ears learn to sometimes hear a cry for help or a warning, but mostly it's just one a cappella group screeching, screaming, cussing, madness, and misery. And four, the utter insanity of the system. As jailers, you often see the worst of the worst. They eventually move to a prison. Sometimes, you see who we call "frequent flyers." The same people getting arrested for the same things. Then, occasionally you see someone inside that just does not fit or belong. Perhaps they let their license expire or hit someone, maybe a wealthy older female with a DUI. These folks tend to make bail very fast.

You get pretty good at reading the room and the inmates. You can look up to see a new inmate entering the cell block and can guess why they're locked up. You get good at guessing their backgrounds and reasons for their crimes. You get lied to, conned, scammed, and misdirected all the time. You quickly learn never to talk about your life, wear jewelry, make jokes, or do a favor for an inmate. Inmates know the rules and your standard operating procedures better than you do. If you violate a rule or a right, they will file a grievance faster than you can spit.

Carl Patton knew these rules. He knew the consequences of violating the rules. He also knew if he got caught with a cell phone he would take the whole wrap. He'd never snitch on another inmate. Carl Patton lived and would die by the code. He had lived that life on the streets, and he would live it on the inside. His loyalty to what he knew and understood never wavered.

It might be an archaic way of thinking for a lot of people, but I understand the thought. You protect the ones you love and the ones who can't protect themselves. And you never, ever allow anyone to harm them. If somehow they are harmed, there should be a clear and swift response.

Chapter 22

BREAKING HEARTS

I GOT A TEXT FROM Norma that Carl was in the hospital with heart issues. Norma knew something was wrong. She got a notice that their weekly visitation had been canceled. Then she learned that her husband was seriously ill. It seemed so cruel that he would be so ill right as the case was moving forward. Slow, almost tar pitch, but still moving.

I knew he'd be mad. He hated missing Norma's visits for any reason. Once the prison shut down because of a "disturbance," preventing Norma from visiting. Carl was hopping mad for months over it!

Carl was not the only loyal one. Norma drove three hours for a three-hour visit, then three hours back home every week. She made the trip the same way for twenty-five years. I asked her once if she had ever considered divorcing Carl.

She responded quickly with a simple but firm one-word answer. "No." That was the end of that conversation. Later she said, "You know lots of our family didn't think Carl and I would make it. I guess we proved them wrong."

No matter his condition at the hospital, knowing Carl, I knew he was giving the nurses hell. He was most likely demanding to see Norma and get a message to Tina. He wanted to see them and get justice for Melissa.

Tina texted me soon after Norma.

It ain't good,

her text said. I knew she was devoted to her father and wanted to be there with him. They had to wait and see how he fared through the night. Fingers crossed they'd be able to see him the next day. Even tough guys like Carl Patton needed their families.

One of the toughest guys in American history was Sheriff Buford Pusser. Pusser was sheriff of McNairy County, Tennessee, from 1964 to 1970 and has been the inspiration for several movies and books, including the wildly popular movie *Walking Tall.*

Pusser was known to carry a big stick, and he wasn't afraid to use it. Former deputy sheriff and author Mike Elam shared a story about Pusser and one of the inmates in Pusser's jail. According to Elam, Paul David English was in jail for murder. It was Christmastime, and English had told Pusser his momma was in bad health and it might be her last Christmas. To his surprise, on Christmas Day, Pusser took English home to visit his momma. English thought it'd be a quick visit, but he and the sheriff ended up staying all afternoon. They even had dinner!

When they left, Pusser asked English if he wanted to see the famous site where Pusser and his wife, Pauline, were ambushed. It crossed English's mind that Pusser might be taking him out there to shoot him. But after showing him where the shooting happened, Elam said that English told him Pusser said, "Well, you ready to go back to jail?" And that was that. Pusser took him back to jail. It was the last time English would see his momma. If the toughest, meanest, no-nonsense sheriff in American history could let a murderer visit their dying momma at Christmas, surely children should be able to visit a dying parent in the hospital, inmate or not.

August of 2025 Buford Pusser was implicated in his wife's murder. The Tennessee Bureau of Investigation had exhumed Pauline Pusser and investigated her injuries against Pusser's original statements.

The visit from Tina wasn't to be. It's sad when you need your family around you the most and you can't have them there. Even in the hospital, you're still a prisoner. And Carl Patton, the prisoner, wasn't allowed visitors in the hospital. No doubt, Carl had done some truly horrible things, and he deserved to be in prison. I just wish in times like grave illnesses he could have had Norma visit.

Not only did Carl suffer when his family couldn't visit, Norma, Tina, and the grandchildren suffered, too. Imagine knowing your loved one is sitting inside that building and you have to drive past it? Can't go in and see them, talk to them, or hug them. Even knowing the end might be near, you're denied all access. You can't even talk to them on the phone.

Ironic, but it's because of Carl there are children who can't ever talk to their mother, can't hug her, can't hear her laughter. Carl took fathers, sons, brothers, mothers, daughters, sisters, and friends from people who loved them. This ring of sadness has no end. Murder affects generations.

Chapter 23

8 X 10

THE FIRST PHOTOGRAPH OF MELISSA I ever saw was that framed picture her momma was holding the day we met. It looked like a high school graduation picture. Her long brown hair fell softly over her shoulders. She was smiling. She looked sweet and carefree.

So different than what I was at looking now.

Case Number 990798 of the Office of the Medical Examiner: Autopsy of Melissa Wolfenbarger performed by Dr. John B. Parker. Cause of Death: Undetermined. Manner of Death: Homicide.

The reason the cause of death was undetermined is because we didn't know how she was killed. Was she strangled? Stabbed? Shot in the torso? The fact that she was cut into pieces and placed in five different trash bags tells us clearly she was murdered. The report states that her hair was seven to eight inches in length, suggesting that her beautiful brown hair had been cut off. Why would a stranger cut off her hair? That seemed to me like the move of a jealous husband to humiliate his victim.

With everything I'd learned about domestic violence cases, I was very vocal to Norma and Tina about the hair being chopped off. Historically, that type of assault was a known indicator of a very abusive relationship, driven in part by ridicule.

The autopsy was clear that Melissa's "amputation is somewhat roughened but does appear to be the result of the utilization of a saw as opposed to begin 'chopped off' with a sharp instrument." This means the killer took extra time with the victim that wasn't necessary for the murder. If the goal was to kill someone, that's an A to B process. Arguably, a fast event.

This killer took extra time with Melissa, cut her hair off, dismembered her arms and legs, beheaded her, placed her body parts into five separate trash bags, drove her remains to a dumping ground, then disposed of the saw. Nothing in that list had anything to do with the actual killing of her. All those things took place after she was dead.

Wouldn't a stranger kill her and escape as fast as possible? Why would he spend so much extra time with the body? I believe it was because he had to try and hide her. The killer believed if she was never found, people would believe his story about her running away to California.

Carl made the following points: This was not random, this was not a stranger, this was personal, this was overkill, this was a weak attempt to hide her, and Christopher leaving town says it all. Carl said, "I'm surrounded by criminals every day and have been for almost thirty years. None of them would tell you this was a stranger. None."

I thought of that photograph of Melissa often. I wanted it on my wall. Not just any wall. I wanted it on the wall dedicated to the cases we've closed. I wanted to see Melissa's sweet smile smiling back at me from one of Kelly Lawson's beautiful composite drawings.

I looked forward to the day Kelly could draw a stunning picture of Melissa that shows how happy she was. It's important to me when people visit my office and ask about one or more of the faces that stare back at them. As I said, it's my own way of honoring the victims and provides a teaching moment to rookies about how we went about solving their cases. Take the knowledge and skills and pass them on. Use tactics, experts, and creative ways to solve the next one. There will always be a next one, so stay ready.

I'm often asked why I'm so willing to share experts, knowledge, and inventions with folks. This question is baffling to me. I know everyone doesn't share openly. I once received a call from an "expert" who told me for "ten thousand dollars I can solve the Chandra Levy case." I told him he should solve it and best of luck, but I would never pay someone to solve a case. I believe if you have the ability, knowledge, or answers, you should solve it. Get a killer off the street.

Until I could put the composite drawing of Melissa on the closed cases wall, I continued to work her case every day. The case had been literally put on a shelf and forgotten about. It had been pushed to the back of the line more than once because something "more urgent or more important" was happening.

I have asked during the task force meetings where we were on the case, only to be told "we are still interviewing people." What people? Who? How was the case getting stronger? It seemed like at every turn there was a stall tactic. Why no arrest after all this time?

There is a theme among cold case families. They almost all have an issue with lack of communication from law enforcement. Some detectives make promises like, "I'll call you every two weeks and update you." Those two weeks come and go without any communication. Heads up, rookies—if you're not going to call, don't tell them you're going to. Never make a promise you can't keep. Tell them to call *you* in a month. And answer the phone! Or at least call them back when they do. Then tell them what you have done on the case. Never lie even when your intentions are well meaning. This goes for everyone, not just homicide detectives. I've talked with hundreds of victims, and it's always better to call the families and tell them there is nothing new, no new leads, no new tips, nothing, than to just not call. Text, email, *something* in the form of a communicative event. Let them know you haven't forgotten about them or their loved one. Let them know you are still on the case. Let them know you still care.

You can't investigate a cold case halfway. You *must* be all in. These families have most likely been through several detectives, prosecutors, and DAs already. If they're lucky, they've had their story covered by numerous reporters, television anchors, and journalists of all calibers. The majority of those who show interest start strong, maybe make promises, but eventually, the interest will wane. They'll move on to other cases, other news stories. It's imperative to see the case through. Never bail on the department or families. Most importantly, never bail on the victim!

~

When you put on that badge and take the law enforcement oath, you're signing up for varying shifts. You'll work days, nights, weekends, and holidays. And when you're a crime scene investigator, you'll work when you're called out. You get used to it. So, you learn to grasp those moments of downtime and enjoy the little things like spending time in your own backyard.

Walt and I have worked hard to create our own private sanctuary. We have our own oasis with a flowing creek, a lake, and a yard filled with animals and blooming flowers. The deer visit every night. We've also played host to owls, geese, turtles, bats, foxes, and once a swan.

Saturday, April 6, 2024, was one of those days when I was relishing in the downtime. The Masters was coming up and right on cue, the azaleas and irises were in full bloom across Atlanta. One of four major men's annual golf tournaments, the Masters pumps an estimated $120 to $140 million into Augusta's economy. The tournament generates tourism, jobs, and a certain *electricity* throughout the state. It's Georgia's chance to shine. And, honey, I like my own yard to shine like it's dressed up in its Sunday go-to-church clothes. I like for my yard to match Augusta. Well, at least my azaleas.

A cool breeze came off the lake as I was enjoying the back deck, assessing what needed to be done next in the yard.

At 11:26 a.m., my phone rang from a South Georgia number. I couldn't get my gardening gloves off fast enough to answer. Seconds later, I got a notification I had a voicemail. Carl had left me a message. I waited for a callback.

At 11:29, the second call came. I answered and heard that slow, gruff voice.

"Ms. Sheryl, it's Carl Patton."

Although Carl Patton was a bona fide serial killer, I was thrilled to hear his voice. He sounded healthy. He wasted no time and asked me if I'd heard anything about Melissa's case.

I said, "How are you feeling?"

He said, "I'm fine. My heart went down to twenty beats, and they were gonna shock me but didn't have to."

He asked again about Melissa's case. Catching her killer was his priority. Her murder was more important than his health. I told him I'd heard they were going to cover it at our task force meeting on the coming Thursday. "I believe this will be the meeting where they decide if they have enough to go to the DA. They need to ask for permission to take this case to the grand jury. It's time."

In a crazy twist of coincidence, Carl was up for parole that Thursday. Jokingly, I said, "They'll have to let you out 'cause I don't think they want Christopher walking into prison with you still there!"

Carl chuckled, then he said low and slow, "I'm retired; I'm out of the outlaw business. I only want to fish and go to church with Norma." There was a wistfulness to his voice, like someone sharing a daydream.

I have to admit, the hope in his voice tugged at my heart a little. I didn't believe the parole board would have the same feelings. They'd denied him once, and I didn't see this time being any different. I didn't believe they'd ever let him out.

A few days later, I got a text from Norma. I hear you talked to Carl. She must have finally been able to see him on Sunday during their normal visit.

I told her he sounded great. We talked about the task force meeting regarding Melissa's case going to the grand jury. And also about Carl's parole hearing and how both would be on Thursday, April 11, 2024. It would be a big date for the Patton family. If not both, I prayed at least one of the events would come out in their favor. Melissa's case deserved to be heard in a court of law. Her killer needed to face the same punishment as Carl.

Chapter 24

CHECK ALL TRAPS

APRIL 10, 2024, I GOT an email from the DA's office advising that our Cold Case Task Force meeting had been canceled. Yet another postponement for this family. No matter what the world thought about Carl and Norma Patton, their oldest daughter Tina Mae was innocent in the family drama. She was a child when her parents committed their crimes.

Tina was a victim from all sides here. She came to accept that her father was a killer and he most likely would spend the rest of his life in prison. To the world, he was known as the Flint River Killer, or Carl Patton, serial killer. To Tina, he was still known as Daddy. She knew the truth about her mother's involvement with the murders. She knew what the world thought about that, too. How some say Norma should also have been in prison.

Tina also had to live every day knowing someone murdered her sister. In a brutal, horrific way. For many years, she wasn't able to see her niece and nephew. The side reality is she lost a brother-in-law. Tina was a true victim in this murder. On some level she lost her entire family.

The world may think the Patton family wasn't worthy of all the effort to bring justice for Melissa. All the time and resources used when her daddy was sitting in prison for five murders. And her momma helped him. It's the world's prerogative to think what they want. I can't say if they're wrong or they're right.

What I can say is with every cold case, there's a killer out there pumping gas next to you, eating at the table beside you in a restaurant, coaching your son's team, working with your teenage daughter, drinking at a bar with your college-age nephew, renting a room from your brother and his family, or cutting your elderly parents' grass.

No matter what the world felt about him, Carl Patton was necessary to this case. One, he was Melissa's father and deserved to be heard and consulted. Two, his friends were criminals. He understood committing crimes and getting away with them on a level most of us never will. Three, he was a convicted killer.

As an investigator, it's imperative I utilize all experts. Bring in all the experts! Don't be afraid of someone smarter than you. Be grateful they exist and are willing to help you. Learn what they know and then, guess what? You are brilliant, too!

Make no mistake: Carl Patton was an expert. He understood murder on a level I couldn't. He not just killed, he murdered. He also had a family member murdered. His intel was a gift for any investigator or detective. You just needed to get past the fact that he was a killer and get to the place where he had the knowledge and experience you needed. You'll never find the insight Carl offered in a textbook. What he had to teach was powerful.

Back in the day, before you could run down to the grocery store to pick up something for supper, hunters put out various traps to try and catch their food for the coming days and fur for warmth during the cold winter months. Some traps were close to their cabin, but many were miles away. After all, what you're hoping to trap probably isn't going to show up on your front doorstep. So, you walk miles in the snow and it's tough, tiring, and often rendered no results. Imagine hiking through the bitter cold, with snow above your knees, and coming upon your trap—and it's empty.

Working cold cases will be tough. You will get tired, and your efforts will often render no results. Sound familiar? Like the hunter, the more traps you put out requires more work, but more traps improves your odds of hitting a positive result. Check all your traps, because that one payoff will make all the failures worth it. You won't dwell on the empty traps in the years to come, you'll only highlight the successes in the story!

Carl and I put out several traps during the investigation. One of the first was the media. We utilized it every way we knew how. We used local news stations, social media, and speeches to try and locate anyone who witnessed Christopher's abuse toward Melissa. Eventually, that trap expanded to include national media, podcasts, and platforms like CrimeCon.

The second trap was to locate something in the case file not utilized by police. After reviewing front to back, left to right, upside down and sideways, I told Carl I thought I found the target. In Melissa's case file, I found these forms and notes:

1. From the Office of the Solicitor General of Fulton County Investigations Division, regarding a domestic violence case. It's a handwritten note, dated January 5, 1998, from Allison Byrd stating, "Please personally serve victim today—so service will be good for Thursday." Another form dated January 6, 1999, was a Proof of Service form where an investigator checked the box that he did "a diligent search for Melissa Wolfenbarger" and was unable to locate her to serve her with a subpoena. The address listed is 824 Brookline Street, SW Atlanta, Christopher and Melissa's home. Christopher Wolfenbarger was listed as the defendant and Melissa was listed as the witness.

How did Christopher respond to the charges? Did he allow the charges to be dismissed since the victim was not in court? Did he tell the court that Melissa ran off to California? What excuse was given for the victim not being in court on a domestic violence case? Why would they accept his explanation in such a case when *he* was the accused?

2. From the Office of the Solicitor General of Fulton County Request for Investigation. It's dated January 6, 1998, and listed as needed January 7, 1998. Christopher Wolfenbarger is listed as the defendant. The line for Charges states: "Simple Battery /

> I will upgrade to Battery." Case Number 213831. In the section listed Information Needed: "Rhonda—Please personally serve victim Melissa Wolfenbarger at the address you obtained from her mother on 1-5-98." On the back of the form handwritten it states: "Victim is on DeKalb Probation. Oz checked NCIC and GCIC on 1-7-99 and could not find no outstanding warrants on victim. 10-6-98 DeKalb Co. Sheriff's Department issued warrant for Probation Violation on victim."

I knew Oz. He was a top-notch investigator. Oz Armour and I worked together forty years ago when I worked for the solicitor general. We worked together again about twenty years ago for the board of regents for campus safety for all University of Georgia colleges. If Oz could not find her, that was pretty telling.

3. The last document in this series may say the most. It's listed as Motion and Order to Place Case Upon the Dead Docket. The handwritten note on the form says: "Unable to locate victim. Warrant Case. V in violation of Probation for Not reporting." Dated, March 15, 1999.

Did no one think to ask where she might be? Was there no cause for concern? They knew she had small children. There was a rumor circulating that she might be pregnant. A victim in a domestic violence case suddenly stops coming to court, is not at her home, and fails to report to her probation officer and not one person in the system thinks to contact police or her family? They could locate her mom for an updated address but didn't try to locate Norma when Melissa went missing? By not reporting Melissa missing, Christopher allowed his wife, the mother of his children, to have a bench warrant taken out on her. If she was in California or *anywhere*, he was willing to let her get arrested for a probation violation. Carl and I agreed that people would see, at the very least, a piece of shit, and at the very most a killer.

Chapter 25

YOUR OWN ZONE 7

EVERYONE WON'T MAKE IT INTO your inner circle. They ain't supposed to. Everyone won't get you. They won't understand you. Everyone can't see your vision. That's fine. It's your vision and they're wrong, so don't waste time trying to convince them otherwise. Thank them for their time, let them go, and move on. They're needed elsewhere, so don't hold them up.

One time when I was a guest on Nancy Grace's show, one of the other guests was a well-respected and smart criminal profiler. Nancy asked my assessment of the crime scene and who I thought was responsible. I gave my answer without hesitation. I believed I was right.

The well-respected profiler was next up and said, "I agree with half of what Sheryl said."

Laughing, I said, "Well then, you're only half wrong!" Of course I was joking. Kinda. There's truth in humor.

When you're hired for a job, whether it's a first job or your tenth, you know who you are working for. You know who your employer is. Who you're working *with* is a whole different ball game. If you're lucky, you might get to select who you work with. Most of the time, that's not how it works. You don't get to select who you work with any more than you get to choose whose case you work.

That's when it becomes imperative that you select your team, your circle, and your outside family carefully. The most important decisions I have made in my career have been the who. Not when we became tight, not why, not how, not what, not where, but *who.*

I tell my own children that I respect people with the guts to put it all on the line. Folks like Oprah, Ellen, and Carol Burnett—all three had their shows titled with their own name. They had guts.

Now, I love me some Carol Burnett. *The Carol Burnett Show*, a variety/sketch/comedy show named after its star, ran on CBS from 1967 to 1978. Many shows during that time were named after the star, or stars. Think *The Mary Tyler Moore Show*, *The Dick Van Dyke Show*, *The Smothers Brothers Comedy Hour*, and so on. Like with Carol Burnett, it was clear who was steering the ship. The success or failure of the show was on her shoulders. So, Burnett did a smart thing: She assembled a team.

Harvey Korman, Tim Conway, and Vicki Lawrence were nothing short of brilliant in their ability to work together. Their chemistry drove them to feed off one another, leading to some of the funniest sketches ever seen on television. And often, bloopers didn't stop the cameras from rolling. That's when the real magic happened—when they cracked one another up. If you haven't seen the sketch when Conway plays the dentist and Korman's the patient, look it up. You'll laugh till you cry. I promise.

That sketch didn't even feature Burnett. She took a step back out of the spotlight and let her team shine. That's called respect. She respected her team members' ability and honored them with trust that they wouldn't let her down. That kind of trust allows humor and heroics.

My sister Shelley has always been supportive and an active participant in my life. She, like Carol, revels in the successes of me and my other three sisters. She taught me by example: Take care of your people.

That sentiment was never more evident than the 1996 Summer Olympics. For the first time in Atlanta's history, the city hosted the Olympics. Unfortunately, it wasn't all fun and games.

It was after midnight on Saturday, July 27. I'd just gotten home after a fantastic day on duty at the games. I was tired, but still feeling little twinges of the adrenaline rush of just being there—at the freakin' Olympics! Practically in my own backyard. I'd just begun to relax when two pagers and a cell phone that I carried started all going off at the same time. I knew this wasn't a drill.

At approximately 1:20 a.m., a bomb had exploded in Olympic Park. At that time, I oversaw the Crisis Response Team. All four of my sisters also volunteered on the team. We had received reports that we had 111 injured and one dead at the scene from shrapnel. One died at the hospital from a heart attack.

We got the whole team together and immediately went to work. We contacted every victim at every metro hospital, interviewed all witnesses on scene, and set up the command center. We were all in rapid response mode.

Then like a slow-motion movie, in walks my sister Sheila and her wife Deedy with breakfast and drinks for everyone. She thought of a mainstay, a staple that we had not. In those moments, having something to eat and something to drink was a source of not only comfort but of necessity. Don't forget to take care of your people. They're your team.

My team, including my sisters, my husband, and my children, plus my work team, will tell you I've never been a halfway person with anything I love and believe in. If I'm in, I'm all in. Family, marriage, children, a case, a game! If you approach things with an all-in attitude, you're invested at a higher degree. You'll hear some of the great investigators proclaim "my case!" Because that's how they work it. They feel the ownership and they claim it. I'll tell you right now Melissa Wolfenbarger was my case. I proclaimed it and I claimed it.

With marriage, a friendship, a job, or a case, once you've proclaimed it, you treat it with the respect it deserves. You work your ass off for it, and you remain loyal to it. Carl Patton and I agreed on that major life principle—loyalty! You're always there no matter what they've done, what they're going through, or what they may need. Walt has shown me loyalty since I was fourteen. For me his loyalty feels like a homebase. A lighthouse. A guidepost. Carl saw loyalty as a protective shield. For twenty-five years Norma kept his biggest secret. She stood by him. Fed him. Kept their home and raised their children. And when he went to prison, she continued to stand by him. Divorce never crossed either of their minds. There was no mystery to their loyalty.

But there were plenty of mysteries that still surrounded Melissa's case. One, we didn't know where Melissa was killed. Or even how she was killed. Two, we didn't know where she was dismembered and beheaded. Three, we didn't know which vehicle was used to transport her remains to the dump site. And four, we still didn't know where her torso was.

We didn't have to know these things to convict the killer. It would have been nice to have all the answers, but that's not realistic or needed. We could go forward with the facts and evidence we did have and paint a picture that would either fill in those blanks or show they were not essential. The bottom line for me was if the killer wanted to help the family or himself, they would have come forward with the answers. Carl did. He manned up and took full responsibility for his crimes. I couldn't see Christopher doing the same thing. But I could always hope.

Chapter 26

ARE WE THERE YET?

WHENEVER I DO A SPEECH on a cold case and lay the case out to the room of participants, I think of them as my jury. If at the end of the speech they have tons of questions and seem to not have fully grasped the dots that I believe I've connected, then I know I have work to do. But if that room feels angry at the injustice, are mad at the system, see the same suspect as I do—then I know I'm on the right track. And every now and then I will have a guest who has an idea on how to solve a case. And it's good. I get pushback from veteran detectives sometimes about having civilians weigh in on cases, but I'm here to tell you anyone can solve a cold case.

Don't get me wrong: I'm not diminishing the hard work, years of training, and experience investigators put into working a cold case. But an extra set of eyes never hurts. Even if those eyes belong to a civilian.

The Zodiac code was broken by a schoolteacher sitting at his dining room table. The DC Sniper was found by a trucker. The cold case of Jacob Wetterling was solved by a blogger and another victim. There are many more instances where everyday people have solved cases. Once I was chastised by a high-ranking officer who said in part, "I can't believe you of all people are allowing civilians off the street to 'investigate' a cold case."

I said, "Well, I guess when I saw you last week hanging up a BOLO sign, it was only for law enforcement driving by." The only thing I heard after that were crickets.

Law enforcement knows civilians are a vital part of cases. Even when the civilian is a victim's parent sitting in prison. Carl may have never finished high school, but don't be fooled by the lack of a diploma. He understood the importance of media and posting on social media. And at the time, it was the only thing that kept Melissa's case alive.

Carl and I often talked about the media using him as a pawn to gain more attention for Melissa's case. Although he hated the moniker "the Flint River Killer," he understood how it could help. We agreed that events like CrimeCon, places like the Georgia Writers Museum, and people like Nancy Grace were interested because of the hook of the Flint River Killer. Carl was smart enough to know it was *his* past that drew attention to Melissa's case. Like it or not, that's just how it was. If the media and others wanted to use his background to help catch Melissa's killer, so be it.

Did whoever tied those bags murder Melissa? It would take more than a general expert to extract the DNA from the bags, and I had the number of one of the best in the world in my phone. I called Francine Bardole and asked her opinion about the knots used to tie the bags. From an evidentiary standpoint, they were the best option for recovering DNA from the killer. They'd been tied tight, and the inside of the knots might have been the area most protected from the elements like rain, heat, snow, wind, cold, and animal activity. I was hoping at one time the five different bags were piled on top of each other, thereby shielding the ones in the middle. Francine was the best in her field, and I knew if anyone could help, she could.

Francine mentioned consulting with another DNA expert, Suzanna Ryan. I'd worked with both analysts on another cold case where unusual items had yielded usable DNA. The problem with bringing in experts lies in a universal truth—money. Or lack thereof. Not that Francine and Suzanna wouldn't volunteer their time, but the testing itself can run into high dollars.

I wasn't going to let something like money derail the quest for justice in Melissa's case. I went to Adriane Love and explained my idea on how we could get the testing paid for. I told her I'd been successful in the past helping law enforcement raise and apply for funds in other cases. Believe it or not, most of these funds, if not all of them, came from everyday people. Donations, fundraising events, and benefactors willing to share their good fortune. These outsiders stepped in and changed the game. If it weren't for the generosity of strangers and caring public, many cases would not be solved today. It's vile to think a person's freedom is at stake and money becomes a factor. It's equally as putrid when justice for an innocent victim is at stake and money becomes a factor.

Although it was still April, Hotlanta was living up to its nickname. A wave of hot air hit me in the face when I opened the door to my CSI truck. It was a sunny, beautiful day, but I wasn't ready for the summer heat yet. I climbed in, cranked the engine, and adjusted the air-conditioning. The cold air was welcome as I radioed to hold me out. I was headed to the Roswell Police Department Cold Case Task Force meeting.

I was excited the meeting was finally going to happen. I was anxious to hear the progress the district attorney's office had made on Melissa's case. I was prepared and eager to share whatever I could. We were close; I could feel it. Even the Atlanta traffic couldn't diminish my excitement.

As I walked into the room, I saw Detective Summer Benton. In addition to being an excellent detective, she's a wonderful person. I was thrilled to see her and looked forward to hearing commentary on several of our task force cases. I sat down next to her, and we started chatting about her recent episode on *Zone 7*. The feedback I had gotten put Summer at celebrity status. She was a bona fide rock star!

Her approach to solving cases mirrors mine in that we are global in our approach. Nothing should be left out or untried. We both investigated by the mantra "every tool on every case every time."

After reviewing a few cases, Deputy District Attorney Vincent Faucette finally got to Melissa. He said they were having a difficult time getting the information regarding Christopher's confession to his mother's preacher. In Georgia, as with attorneys and doctors, conversations with clergy are considered privileged. Faucette added that they thought about having the preacher call Christopher, but I was told the pastor's wife nixed that idea.

My disappointment was real. It was unfortunate we couldn't use the confession. The preacher could have been the key to breaking Melissa's case wide open. All it would have taken was a simple call from the preacher saying, "Hey Christopher, I was just checking on you since our conversation years ago. How have you been since you killed Melissa?" Well, I know it wouldn't have gone exactly like that, but a gal can hope. Proverbs 24:25: "But it will go well with those who convict the guilty, and rich blessing will come on them."

Faucette went on to talk about Christopher's mother and sister, referring to them as the mother and sister of the *suspect*. He said they'd told investigators, "Every time Melissa would run off, Christopher would track her down and bring her back."

Then why didn't he do that this time? Why did he never look for her? Why didn't he demand police action? Seems to me any loving husband would be beating down the doors at the police station. Why didn't he ever call the police with tips and theories or asking for an update? Why did he take his and Melissa's children to the wrong cemetery to see where their mommy was buried? Yeah. He did that, too. Real peach of a guy.

Faucette continued, stating they were trying to get Melissa's medical records but had failed. So, Faucette said, they were going to try and contact Norma to get Melissa's insurance carrier at the time she went missing. They needed to know once and for all if Melissa was pregnant. I piped up and said I could be some help with that.

I told the room of task force members there was no way Melissa had insurance. She barely worked, and when she did it was often low-level jobs with no benefits. With no health insurance, the local health department would have been where Melissa would have gone for medical issues.

Sharing that type of information in situations such as this isn't being harsh or mean. It's not gossiping about those less fortunate or who may not have the means to pay for medical care. It's standard victimology. And it was Melissa's victimology. It's imperative we understand the victim before we can zero in on a viable suspect. It saves time when we're trying to track down information, and it shows a jury who the victim was.

Everyone in the room agreed this was a circumstantial case. But we had gotten a true bill from the grand jury with less. New evidence would be great, but the reality was one witness had already died, and waiting only increased the chance of losing other witnesses and evidence.

Even though the preacher couldn't testify about the content of his conversation with Christopher, he *could* testify that Christopher came to talk with him. He could also describe his observations about Christopher's demeanor and how he was acting. Was Christopher sweating, pacing, scared, or anxious? The preacher could share that. The jury could infer the rest.

You know how you can feel things in your bones? I was feeling it. We were close. *So* close. All we needed was the deputy district attorney and the district attorney to sign off and take Melissa's case to the grand jury. I miss the good ol' days when district attorneys had the power to take a case they believed in and run with it. All the political jockeying and wanting to only take a case they can win is infuriating.

Consider what happens when someone is accused of a crime. It's one of two things: Either people come out of the woodwork in disbelief and support that person, or other victims come out. Think about the rape cases against Kobe Bryant or the Duke lacrosse team. First, no other victims came forward. Second, they were never accused of rape again. Now consider Bill Cosby. Once he was accused, victim after victim after victim came forward. The spotlight of arrest can be a powerful tool for law enforcement. What happens and what doesn't happen helps paint a picture of the accused. Think of Bryan Kohberger. He was arrested for the murder of four college students. Not one student, coworker, preacher, neighbor, boss, professor, high school friend, lover, or roommate has come forward to say there's no way Bryan did this crime. Not one person stood up for his character. Not one.

Chapter 27

STOLEN MOMENTS

IT WAS SATURDAY, APRIL 20, 2024. My sister Sharlene and I were out shopping for baby gifts for our niece Zoe. She was pregnant with her first child, so we were driving from store to store, hunting for perfect gifts. My daughter, Caroline, had texted me earlier. I told her Sharlene and I were shopping in the town next to hers. After hearing where we were, Caroline texted, I'm coming to meet y'all and surprise Lene.

Sharlene and I were throwing Zoe a surprise shower in Florida where our other sister, Sheila, lived. Sheila was in the middle of chemo treatments, and we wanted her to be able to attend the shower. Sharlene has a second home in the Sunshine State, so we always have a place to stay when we visit Sheila. Being this was yet another bout of cancer for Sheila, we wanted to visit as often as we could. Having a house available anytime made that possible. We were beyond fortunate; we were blessed.

It was 3:56 in the afternoon when my phone rang. It was a South Georgia area code, so I didn't answer. I waited for the second call to come immediately after. That was our pattern. Let the phone ring once, then hang up and call right back.

I answered the second time he called. "Ms. Sheryl, it's Carl Patton."

I told him he sounded great after being in the hospital a second time.

He assured me, "I'm gonna live to be a hundred."

I just hoped he lived long enough to see his daughter's killer behind bars. I brought him up to speed on the Cold Case Task Force meeting I'd attended two days earlier. I explained that the team was still working on Melissa's case. Carl had heard that so many times already, I hesitated to even say it. But at least they were working it. Like a cheerleader, I told him the task force was checking items off their list. They wanted to find a few more witnesses and perhaps locate Melissa's insurance provider.

I heard his low grunt. I told him how I explained to the group that she likely didn't have insurance, and their best bet would be the health department, although I doubted they held on to records for thirty years.

Carl's voice was low and defeated. He spoke slowly. "She didn't have insurance."

It was one of those moments when I knew he realized the people in charge of prosecuting his daughter's case don't know basic information about her.

Carl had told me once his favorite picture of Melissa was the "red, white, and blue one." It looked like one of those Glamour Shots pictures. Long before everyone's phone had a camera with filters, there was Glamour Shots. The photo studios were in malls across the country and offered photo sessions with stunning results. After a personal consult with a style pro, the team went to work. The makeover included hairstyling, makeup, wardrobe, and accessories. Think big hair, bigger jewelry, and loud, colorful clothing. Back in the '80s and '90s, Glamour Shots and its many imitators were all the rage. Women couldn't make their appointments fast enough. They wanted that one photo that made them look like a movie star.

Melissa had been no different. Her beautiful smile was framed by her long brown hair with cascading curls around her face. She wore an American flag leather jacket and big red flower earrings. Her deep, dark eyes reflected her kindness. Her hands held the lapels of the jacket. She looked so happy. She wasn't wearing her wedding band in the photo.

That picture is part of her victimology. I wondered if other members of the task force had even taken the time to understand it. To know what was going on in her life then and when she went missing?

I had felt the frustration in Carl's voice when he said Melissa didn't have insurance. I understood. I changed the subject to his upcoming parole hearing.

His voice lifted a little. "I feel good about it."

Carl wanted to go home. He wanted Christopher in prison. It was so hard to wait on the actions of others. I wish I could have just taken the reins and gotten a team together and located all the witnesses and needed paperwork that was out there and gone to the grand jury. I couldn't wrap my brain around how Carl must have felt. Powerless. Completely powerless. I'd lose my mind.

Except for that one incident when he'd slugged Christopher, Carl had stayed clean and crime-free for twenty-five years. He'd made a good career out of his carpentry and roofing experience. After he was sentenced to life behind bars, Carl had done everything the prison asked of him. He tried to add things of value to his life like furthering his education and earning job trade certificates. He took classes, stayed out of trouble, mentored new young inmates, and worked various jobs.

If he ever did earn parole, Carl wanted to rebuild his life. I knew it was possible. I've watched the phenomenon from the front row. My sister Shelley rebuilt her life over and over and over again. With each setback she rebuilt stronger than she was before. Each time, she'd gained more tools to help her master the rebuilding process. Shelley's lost a child, divorced, lost jobs, moved, gone back to school, started a business, and most recently and most impressively learned to walk again following a horrific accident.

Carl and I talked often about his life once the gates opened for him. He always stopped me before we got too far into the good stuff and said, "First I want to help put Melissa's killer in prison."

Before we hung up, I told him I'd keep Norma updated with anything I heard, and she could brief him when she visited on Sundays. Although the call had ended, my thoughts of Carl and Melissa didn't.

Caroline was driving half an hour from her apartment to meet us and surprise Sharlene. I thought about how this simple act was going be the highlight of the day for the three of us. When my children, Huck and

Caroline, were little I taught them these pleasant little occurrences were "stolen moments," a time when you weren't supposed to see the person but a chance meeting or a quick altered plan makes the meeting happen. It's a gift, fate, a stolen moment. I see it as a reward of extra time. Running into an old classmate from twenty years ago, seeing a neighbor at a ball game, seeing your old teacher at the gas station or your sister at the grocery store. You just stole some extra time. A moment not of chance but a gift. A moment to add a laugh, a hug, or an extra "I love you." A God-given donation to your life.

Not that he didn't deserve to be where he was, but it made me think how Carl didn't have those gifts of stolen moments. Everything was planned for him: when he eats, bathes, or sees Norma. No chance meetings, sightings, or reunions.

When Huck and Caroline were little, I would always kiss them goodnight twice. My feeling was if I was ever not there to kiss them, they had one in the bank. And for me, I felt like I was cheating time by double loving on them. It's an ever-present reality when I'm working a homicide how so many people get cheated out of a little more laughter, more events, and more love.

Melissa Wolfenbarger was cheated. The most beautiful things in life were ripped from her. Her two children, Christina and Joey, are the biggest victims in this case. The massive loss they can't even conceptualize. People always want to talk about the big moments loved ones aren't there for, but I contend that everyday things are even more significant. Yes, the absence of a loved one at the monumental events like graduations, weddings, and the birth of babies is a terrific, painful loss. That first Christmas without them just isn't quite the same. That first Mother's Day without your mother is a different kind of sad.

But those Tuesday night car rides, singing a favorite song, cracking up to an inside joke, and dancing in the kitchen moments are even more debilitating when that person isn't there. Melissa's children never got to know her, drive in the car and sing along to the radio with her, crack up over their own inside joke, or dance with her in the kitchen.

Chapter 28

DIESEL THERAPY

APRIL 24, 2024, I HEARD the soft ping of my phone notifying me I had a text message. I looked down and saw it was from Norma. At 8:53 p.m. It wasn't terribly late, but late enough to raise a concern. Call me when you can. Carl is being transferred, don't know where.

Transferred? Why? Was this because of his ongoing medical issues? His parole? Or was it punishment?

Even Carl didn't know. He'd called Norma and told her he was being transferred and that's all he knew. Norma was worried they were going to move him farther away. She had no idea why this was happening. She had to call Tina and tell her, but she hated the thought of that. Tina would want to know where, why…and Norma didn't know what to tell her.

April 25; 2024, at 7:53 a.m., I was waiting for the prison inmate search to update Carl's new prison address. Once we knew what facility he had been moved to, we might be able to piece together why he was sent to another prison in the first place.

I explained to Norma if he had been told at night that he was leaving first thing in the morning, that wouldn't have been for punishment. For that, they would have grabbed him and put him on a bus in the middle of the night. In the world of corrections, the term for moving a troublesome inmate is "diesel therapy." Basically, it's putting that inmate on a bus and moving them far away to another facility.

I believed he was being transferred for medical reasons. Carl had been in and out of the hospital several times in the last few weeks. Most wardens wouldn't take a chance on an inmate being sick and not taking the steps to make certain he got the treatment he needed. Moving them to another facility better equipped to handle their medical issues made perfect sense. It also reduced the liability of the original facility.

I was with my sisters in Florida driving the car on the beach. It was one of the last places where you could still do that. It was also one of my favorite things to do. Probably because it evoked such happy memories of when I was a little girl. My mother had a convertible, and every evening while we were on vacation, we drove it on the beach.

On this day, the water was especially green and blue, with a strong breeze blowing in from the north. There were more birds than normal. My phone made that familiar ping signifying I had a text message. I glanced down to see it was from Norma. It was one word: Savannah.

Carl had been moved to Coastal State Prison in Savannah, Georgia. It was a medium-security prison with approximately 1,800 inmates. Carl would have to make new friends, new contacts, and new "business associates." Meaning he had to find the person with the cell phone and work out a deal to call me or Norma.

Coastal State Prison also meant he was moved due to his medical condition. It was good he would be getting the medical care he needed, but it also meant he'd be farther away from Norma and Tina. Rather than a six-hour round trip every Sunday, Norma would now have to make a ten-hour round trip for a two-hour visit with her husband.

~

What could a killer tell me that I didn't already know? First, Carl confirmed my thoughts on the cause of death. Although we still didn't have the actual cause of death, evidence of Christopher's previous abuse—the bruising seen on Melissa's neck—and his confession gave us what we needed to know: strangulation. That gave us insight into the reason behind the beheading and dismemberment. Carl and I agreed that was how he got her body out of the house unseen but the State would have to prove it. I often had to remind Carl it does not matter what you believe, think, or feel; only what the state can prove.

According to Carl, it's when you're in that "state of self-preservation" that mistakes are made. You start to think about yourself and forget important evidence left behind, or you start to build a story that won't make sense or match the evidence. He said, "Remember, I forgot to get rid of the bloodstained pillow. It might have taken twenty-five years, but they caught me because of it."

The pre- and post-crime behaviors matter. People have patterns, routines, the order they do things in. When those patterns are broken, altered, or forgone, that's a red flag to me. For example, Christopher had never let Melissa leave him without going after her. Except this time, she tells him that she's going to California. And he's okay with it. He even drops her off at the train station. Why the change in his pattern? Melissa had always kept in touch with her momma on her birthday. Why didn't she call that time? And why didn't she call and tell her all about California? Like Carl said, Christopher's story wasn't making sense.

I knew just the person who could help us make sense of it: our Cold Case Task Force member, Detective Summer Benton. Summer's a smart, streetwise, and polite homicide detective. She's a local celebrity because of her stint on *The First 48* and the local news. She understood that having the pulse of the street and a willingness to work with anyone who could help your case was important.

Summer is also pretty and soft spoken, but there's an undercurrent of bravery ever present. You knew not to let her petite frame fool you. Summer could take care of herself. Her daddy is a well-respected former cop. They talk shop when she needs advice on a case.

Summer and I saw Melissa's case the same way. We shared the same theories and worked them in the same manner. Once Christopher was arrested, and I felt certain the time was drawing near, I thought Summer would be the best person to interview him. It was a tactic, but I'd seen it work time and time again. The soft-spoken, caring female who understood that he loved his wife. That knowing and understanding that he didn't mean to kill her. Summer believed this and could legitimately show care and concern for what happened in that house on that fateful day in December.

I needed to reach out to Summer and tell her that they moved Carl to Savannah. I believed once Christopher was in custody, someone from the Atlanta Police Department or the DA's office should tell Carl in person. Regardless of what he'd done in the past, he was Melissa's father, and he deserved that. Detective Summer Benton would be a gentle source of that information.

Chapter 29

HAND TO GOD MOMENTS

I OFTEN TALK ABOUT THE Hand to God moments working these cold cases. On every single investigation, I can point to a moment so saturated with higher-power pilotage that it can't be ignored. April 29, 2024, for sure was one of those days.

Norma was having a difficult time. Carl had been moved farther away, making it harder for her to visit. He was her partner. He was her husband. For better or for worse. The two hours a week she was allowed to see him gave her just enough strength to get through the next week.

She texted me at 8:39 that morning. Twenty-five years ago, her head was found, and twenty-one since I buried her. A hard day for me. And Carl being moved doesn't help because now I don't have a day to look forward to for our visit.

My heart ached for her. No mother should ever have to bury a child. Regardless of that child's age. Despite the pain Norma was feeling that day, beyond all the heartache, there was a Hand to God moment I couldn't wait to share with her.

Before the text message from Norma, I had received a Facebook instant message at 8:18 that morning. The message read: Hi Sheryl, I was curious if you're still working on Melissa Wolfenbarger's case… If so, I would like to talk with you about it if you have time.

I immediately sent my cell phone number and received an incoming call nine minutes later. I spoke with the caller for approximately eighteen minutes and then drafted a letter to Deputy District Attorney Faucette using my notes from the call.

This is the email I sent to DDA Faucette at 9:32 a.m.:

> DDA Faucette,
>
> Today April 29, 2024 at approximately 8:18 AM I received a Facebook message from a young lady who wants to remain anonymous.
>
> She stated: I would like to talk with you about Melissa Wolfenbarger's case.
>
> I sent her my phone number, and soon after she called.
>
> She stated in part: I spent a lot of time with Chris and I always got the feeling he was not to be messed with. He once cornered me and he scared me.
>
> She said Christopher was the oldest in their old friendship group then went on to say: Chris used to be with Crystal and once at a party, they were kinda fussing and he pressed her up against a wall, kinda just with his body and he said you know what happened to my first wife. She went on to say, I have no doubt he was involved with what happened to Melissa.
>
> She continued: Chris cheated on Crystal with Kara. Kara was married to our friend Jonathon. I was deposed during their divorce because I had proof on my phone of the affair.
>
> She stated Jonathon is now deceased, then continued: The investigators should talk to Crystal Autrey. They have a kid together, Ailas, she either lives in Locust Grove or in Orchard Hills where Chris lives. Crystal has deleted all of her social media. But she knows about Chris's abuse.

> Kara Samples is still with Chris. He is on her Facebook profile, but she is Kara Renee on Facebook.
>
> She believes Chris may have Dixie Mafia ties because he got away with Melissa's murder and back when they all used to street race, he never got a ticket because of his ties with the Atlanta Police Department.
>
> She concluded our call by saying Kara was afraid of Chris and she wants to be anonymous because she is scared of him, too.
>
> I told the caller I would contact you and that your investigator might contact her. I told her I would also send a message to Det. Summer Benton. She agreed to speak with you or your designated person. The phone number she can be reached at is [xxx xxx xxxx].
>
> I thanked her for reaching out.

After I hit send on the email, I couldn't stop thinking about the timing of the call. Why today? Why after a decade would this brave witness decide to contact me today? I believed it was divine intervention. I believed Norma needed this that day. I believed the timing was as it should be.

It was close to 1:00 p.m. when I received a reply from DDA Faucette.

> Hi CSI McCollum,
>
> Good Morning. Thank You for passing this information along to us. We will reach out to her.

At 1:05 p.m., Detective Jarion Shephard called me on my private cell phone. He was excited about this witness that Detective Benton had shared with him as well as the email that was forwarded to him from DDA Faucette.

He thanked me profusely for the information and then asked if I thought the witnesses would talk with him. I assured him she would. She was afraid of Chris and didn't want to give her name but wanted to share the information she'd held on to for a decade. Shephard asked for the caller's number and said he'd call her as soon as we hung up. I could tell by the tone of his voice he was eager to speak with her.

Detective Shephard's reputation preceded him. He's a devoted and solid detective. "Call her back and tell her I'm the real deal and I'm calling her now."

I loved it when he said that. Shephard *was* the real deal, and I was so happy he was part of this case. I said, "Yes, sir," then immediately hung up and called the witness back. She was excited that the police were taking her information seriously and wanted to talk with her. I reiterated to her that every nail in this coffin counts!

At 1:41, I received a text message from Shephard.

I spoke with her, thank you for the information!

I sat back and smiled.

It felt like we'd accomplished more in the last five hours than we had in months. It kinda felt like we were starting over.

And now that Carl had been moved, he'd have to start over, too. Make new friends, associates, and relationships with guards. He'd have to learn the hierarchy and the power players in Savannah. Every prison has a chain of command. Not with the guards so much as with the inmates.

It wouldn't take him long to find out who the movers and shakers were, but it would take him a bit more time to earn their trust. Word travels fast among prisoners, so I guarantee you before Carl Patton had his first meal at Savannah, everyone knew he was the Flint River Killer. That would go one of two ways for him: Either other inmates would leave him alone, or some punk would see it as an opportunity to make a name for himself. I hoped they would leave him alone.

The move to a new prison flipped his world upside down, and it also stalled our communication. It would be a while before Carl could prove himself and earn someone's trust to use a contraband cell phone. We were back to letter writing for a while. I couldn't write fast enough to tell him about this new witness.

Since Carl had to start over, I said we did, too. I wanted to start from ground zero and put the case together all over again and get it to the DA for approval for a grand jury. I wanted everyone working the case to get in the same room and lay the details out in bullet points with the corresponding evidence. I wanted to walk a mock jury through the case step by step, day by day, action by action—or in this case, nonaction.

Often, the actions of a suspect are powerful, but their nonactions can be just as powerful, if not more. As I've said, Christopher never once asked the police to find the killer of his wife. He never on behalf of their children demanded justice for her, their mother. In fact, according to Sergeant Layton with the Atlanta Police Department, he stopped cooperating with police.

A few days after the witness came forward, Norma called to tell me Carl was going to try to call me that night. She said, "He's got lots of questions about it for you."

It looked like he'd made "friends" faster than I expected. He already had access to a cell phone.

I remembered parts of a letter he wrote dated October 11, 2022. He said, "The Cherokee and Cheyenne say when you kill something whether animal or human, it becomes a part of you forever and that you never forget. I personally know this to be true. After over 45 years I still remember my actions and sins. Do you think Christopher ever thinks about the mutilation done to Melissa's body?"

I wrote him back and said, "I believe he not only thinks about it, I believe he sees it. Those images will never leave his mind. No matter how much he drinks, no matter how much time has passed, no matter how many new memories are made."

Carl still suffered with visions of his own. And he suffered not because he was in prison. He suffered for the twenty-five years he was free. He had the horrible memories he lived with on top of the looming nightmare that one day the police were going to show up at his door and arrest him. He lived with those thoughts and fears every day. Carl told me more than once that living that way "was a prison" by itself. He was never truly free, and he knew it.

Chapter 30

SETTLE THE SCORE

THE NEXT TIME I TALKED to Carl, I was in Alabama. The big ol' state welcome signs greeted me every time like an old friend. "Sweet Home Alabama" indeed! I love the state sign. My son, Huck, made Alabama his home while attending the University of Alabama as a lacrosse player. I passed that sign many times headed to games or parents' weekend for the Kappa Sigmas. Often Walt and I would burst out singing the lyrics to the song by Lynyrd Skynyrd as we crossed the state line.

It was May 3, 2024, and I'd crossed state lines. My phone rang with a number I didn't recognize from a 912 area code. That's Savannah. I let it go to voicemail. And waited. Sure enough, a second call came right after from the same 912 number.

"Ms. Sheryl, it's Carl Patton."

I was glad to hear from him but surprised. I wasn't expecting a call from him so soon.

He said, "I can't get the phone here like at Dodge. I tried calling you the night before last. It cost me two dollars, and I was dialing the wrong number. This phone belongs to a man that was on the bus with me—he is letting me use it."

I told him Norma had told me he hated it at Savannah. He did. "Ms. Sheryl, they got me in a third world country. I can't get my medication, food, or a phone. It's awful. I was doing great, and they moved me here."

He had told me right before they surprised him with an unrequested move that he'd live to be a hundred. I asked him how he was doing, and I asked him to be honest with me.

Carl started to cry. He said, "The first ten years what keep me going is the thought of getting my hands on him—there ain't a prison where I couldn't find him." After a small pause to collect himself, he continued, "I want him to understand what he has done—done to his kids and whole family."

The call went silent for a moment. The quiet was finally broken by Carl. He slowly and without hesitation said, "He don't know how lucky he is to be alive today. I almost killed him years ago. I blame myself—I should have protected her and I didn't. The only reason I didn't kill him back then is because Norma said Melissa will hate you forever. But at least she'd have her life."

Carl continued, "I want to see him in handcuffs walking into Rice Street…he'll get his ass whooped every day. You know what Rice Street's about—I want to see that on TV."

Carl was correct. I knew Rice Street better than most folks in Atlanta because as I said, I was part of the Fulton County Sheriff's Special Operation Jail Task Force. For almost eight years I worked the Shakedown Team. We would do the raids and searches of the cells looking for contraband: guns, knives, shivs, shanks, drugs, alcohol, and ironically cell phones. Rice Street is rough. But it's also had its share of famous inmates. Like President Donald Trump, but also music producer Phil Spector, rappers Gucci Mane and Scarface, and actor Katt Williams. There are even a few songs that talk about the infamous jail.

Carl said, "I hear you had a phone call about Christopher."

I had wondered what took him so long to ask. I confirmed what he'd heard.

He said, "Norma told me about it, but I want to hear you tell it."

I told him about the entire exchange, the actions I took, and the quick response from the detectives. I told him I believed we were going to see an arrest this month. I thought Detective Shephard would speak with

Melissa and Christopher's daughter, Christina. She'd tell the detective that she wanted her father prosecuted for her mother's murder. That would be powerful testimony on top of the new witness.

He asked what I thought of Shephard. I told him Detective Shephard had been with the Atlanta Police Department about twenty-one years, and nine of those had been in Homicide. He was well respected in his department and outside of Atlanta. He'd been featured on *The First 48*. I trusted Detective Summer Benton, and she said Shephard was one of the best. Carl seemed satisfied that I had all the confidence in the world that we were finally getting somewhere.

Before we hung up, Carl thanked me for everything we were trying to do for Melissa. He then said, "God bless you." Then he ended the call the way he always did. "I can't ever repay what you've done for me and my family."

The sun was shining, and the sky was full of big fluffy clouds that seemed to make the Alabama mountains look small. It's almost an optical illusion. It's stunning and strange all at the same time. Like, how can this be? It made me think of the hypocritical and totally arbitrary treatment of inmates. Who gets special treatment in prison? In 2003, Metallica performed for the inmates at San Quentin State Prison, where they also shot their music video for "St. Anger." But Carl Patton couldn't provide experts with information about his daughter's murder case face-to-face. I'm not advocating for Carl—I'm just saying unequal treatment is never okay. He was locked up and would remain there the rest of his days on earth. That was his punishment. To add extra punishment to a man who'd never broken one of the prison's rules seemed deliberate and unjust.

I often think of my own children when working cases. My son Huck and daughter Caroline are my world. I can't separate what they mean to me and what these parents have clearly lost. I wonder how these parents, these mommas, ever take another breath without their child on this earth. It's unimaginable to put myself in the place of Norma. Your baby girl, your child being murdered and dismembered and left in garbage bags like trash in a junkyard. I know what Carl and Norma did but Melissa deserves someone fighting for her.

This is where Carl and I agreed. Revenge, payback, retaliation—whatever you want to call it, I would want it. I would stand in front of either of my children and take a bullet, fight a bear, or run into a fire without hesitation. The need to avenge any mistreatment of them, whatever that might be, would be too strong to ignore. However slight, I don't believe I would NOT turn the other cheek, nor would I forgive.

I have stood by victims of domestic violence, rape, aggravated assault, and murder. I have done so without fear and without wavering. Most of these victims and their families weren't known to me before our first meeting, often on the crime scene. But there I stood protecting and safeguarding total strangers.

I could understand Carl's desire to kill Christopher. Touch my son or my daughter and I'd want the same thing. Vengeance.

Chapter 31

UPSIDE, DOWN, AND BACKWARDS

MAY 3, 2024, NORMA TEXTED me at noon. "Talked to Faucette, call me when you can." I called her right away and told her I had talked to Carl just a few hours ago.

She said, "Faucette thinks the arrest will happen this month. Shephard has to go and interview Christina and then will put the whole case together and present it for the okay to go and arrest him."

I couldn't fathom the roller-coaster ride of emotions Christina Wolfenbarger was on. To know your father not only killed your mother but dismembered her body. I often think how different Melissa's life would have been if she had never met Christopher Wolfenbarger. If she had met another boy. If she had fallen in love with someone else. I tell my children that if you dance with the devil he will lead. He will spin you around that dance floor as fast as he wants, where he wants, for as long as he wants. But you ain't got to slow dance, tango, or do the lambada; you can line dance, break dance, or do the hustle. I've looked Huck and Caroline straight in the eyes while pointing that momma finger at them and said, "You may be on the dance floor, but you ain't touching."

I've stressed to them to always stay in charge of their movements even during risky or dangerous events. My philosophy? You can work with anyone—just be aware of who you're inviting into your world.

With Shephard interviewing Christina again, and Faucette hoping to make an arrest before the end of the month, I was preparing for a whirlwind of activity in the coming weeks. I'd been asked to give the keynote address at a true-crime conference in June. Various topics ran through my mind, but I kept coming back to one: the importance of utilizing others, even criminals, while working on cold cases. I would narrow it down to what it had been like and what was solidified from working with Carl Patton.

In a rare moment of downtime, I worked on my speech.

The first important thing about working with Carl: Know who you are letting into your circle. I approached Carl as an inmate first. Was he a con artist? Was he trying to use me with the parole board? Did he have a legitimate case, and did he need my help? These are questions I had to ask. Therefore, I had to stay in charge of our interaction. I made up my mind that no matter what he requested, I was in charge. I would question every request and never part from my playbook. I was lead on this investigation and would proceed as I saw fit. The integrity of the investigation, ethics, and results were my call. I set the tone. I would not risk the veracity of the case nor the legitimacy of my own career.

Second, everyone has a gift! Even a serial killer. Regardless of background, past indiscretions, crimes, lack of education, or station in life—everyone has a gift. Now, sometimes we might have to look harder for those gifts, but I promise the gifts are there. When I sent the first letter to Carl, I did so knowing he was a criminal. He was an inmate and had been for decades. I did not completely trust him, and I was certain he didn't completely trust me. But I soon discovered that although he was a con artist and a killer, Carl had the gifts of instinct, loyalty, and leadership.

Third: You can always find common ground. Once you do, rely on that as your foundation of friendship. The common ground does not have to be big like religion or your stance on the death penalty. It can be small like a favorite dish, favorite ball team, or favorite color. Carl and I found common ground over our *family first* approach to everything. I have a saying for my family: "Always All Ways." This simply means I will be there anytime day or night, 24/7, in any way they might need me.

Fourth: Work without fear or favor. I know that when I go to work, I could die. I am fully aware of who I work around every day. So did Carl. He knew the risk he was in every day. I have made it perfectly clear to Huck and Caroline that if I die helping, defending, or seeking justice for another person, I'm good with that. There is no better way to go, in my opinion. I would be irritated if I was hit by a falling tree, or run over by a bus, or struck by lightning. I'd be like, "Saint Peter, are you kidding me, lightning? Is God trying to be funny and ironic? You know what my friends are all going to say when they hear it was a bolt of lightning?" In the line of duty would be an honor. To give my life doing what I love and prayerfully so another could live. The second part, favor—give your time, service, and life's work evenly. Give to others, all others, the best you have. The rewards will be tenfold.

Fifth: Find the experts. No matter who, no matter where, no matter what they are. No one is off limits. Carl Patton was a murderer. He had information I needed that only a killer could provide. If they are famous, smarter than you, or better looking than you—call them anyway. I used to teach college, and that's where I started the Cold Case Investigative Research Institute. I would always tell my students that I wanted to be the dumbest person in the room. If I was the smartest, we would have limitations, and I never wanted limitations. I wanted the best there was on our cases. I have been told no only once. It was an expert who recently was elected to a judgeship, and they could not participate in the investigation due to the rules of their new position. I have used over six hundred experts at the institute. We have done it with no money, no office space, and being volunteer-student driven. People said yes! They said yes for the right reason: to help.

Sixth: Acknowledge the experts. No matter who, no matter where, no matter when—give credit. Thank them publicly, selflessly, and often. The power of a thank-you can be remarkable. The only side note: If an expert is dreadful to you or falls from grace, say nothing. Keep going forward and doing your gig. Unless it's illegal or abusive or criminal, then address them appropriately but not publicly.

Seven: Find your way of investigating. The Jimi Hendrix method. He played his guitar upside down. I investigate upside down and backwards, but just like Hendrix it works. I invented a method and a style that I know works, but more importantly it works for me. The Last 24-361 model is mine. Others have tried to use it for TV shows, articles, and cases, but it ultimately failed because it's not theirs. They are not authentically working a case. If your investigation has no validity, it won't work. The Last 24-361 works for me. You have your own gifts, your own style, and your own way of working a case. Do it that way, and you will be successful.

Back in the early days of the investigation, April 29, 2014, to be exact, I was a guest on Tricia Griffith's podcast *Websleuths*. At the end of her show and off air, I asked if she and her band of citizen sleuths could help me locate the alias Christopher Wolfenbarger allegedly used in Dublin, Georgia. Tricia had built an amazing group of individuals that collectively used their talents to locate people, articles, photographs, evidence, or witnesses. They had assisted me on a few cases and always came through. Carl agreed with me that the more eyes, ears, and hands that are on a case the better.

I always thought Christopher's alias might hold some concealed meaning or key to additional information about his motive, or past behavior. What if the name he used was "Carl"? To add to my suspicion that his aka might hold a key, Christopher had a child with his ex-wife Crystal named Alias. You can't make this stuff up. After his wife goes missing and her body parts are found, he goes on the run using an assumed name, his first wife is determined to be murdered, he has another child…and names him Alias.

Carl and I had talked often about the importance of names and nicknames in the criminal world. For a man who knows he is under a cloud of suspicion for his wife's murder to name a child anything related to getting away with a crime is a massive clue to me regarding his mindset. He thinks he got away with it and is throwing it in everyone's face. That was exactly my feeling. Think about his grin every time someone asked him about the naming of his son.

With Carl being in a new prison with a new warden, I thought I'd try one more time to get permission to visit him. On May 7, 2024, I filled out the paperwork required by the system to be approved by the prison to visit Carl in person. I had to provide my Social Security number, driver's license number, and current address for the background check, and have it all notarized. Then I had to add a letter, also notarized, swearing to the nature of my relationship with Carl.

Chapter 32

TO GET AWAY WITH MURDER

MAY 21, 2024: IT'S 10:00 a.m. when I walk into the Roswell Police Department for the DA's Cold Case Task Force meeting. We're meeting to discuss our cases and their status. I was anxious to hear where we were with Melissa's case. The first point of business from the DA's office was to announce that DDA Faucette would be taking lead on a case that had come back on appeal. The case was against Jonathan Redding of the street gang 30 Deep. My heart literally sank. I wanted to scream, "No! Not again!" They were going to pawn Melissa's case off on yet another new ADA and hold this thing up right here at the finish line. We were so close! It was inconceivable that Melissa would once again take a back seat to a defendant. An already convicted criminal. When would an innocent victim receive justice?

Detective Summer Benton joined the task force meeting via Zoom. She had a case that involved a suspect who stabbed a victim over seventeen times. The subject claimed his penis had been removed and the Queen of England was involved. I told the room I thought Detective Benton should take lead on locating the penis. Through the laptop, Benton came back with, "Mac, that sounds like a field trip for the both of us!"

Everyone in the room laughed. DDA Faucette went on to explain the public defender didn't believe their client was competent to stand trial. Benton yelled, "They're lying!"

Her humor was well established and her instincts and detective work proven.

When we finally got around to Melissa's case, DDA Faucette gave the update. He told the room that a new witness had come forward. I knew it was the witness who had reached out through Facebook after hearing the *Zone 7* podcast. He also said Detective Shephard had interviewed Melissa's daughter, Christina, again.

Christina's statements were downright chilling. She confirmed all the other times her mother would leave her dad that he'd chase her down and bring her back home. That last time, he didn't go after her, and all the family photos of her were removed. The most damning statement came when Christina told Shephard that her dad had told her, "To get away with murder, you have to hide the body parts in different places."

We discussed a few more cases and what tools and avenues could be utilized to move them forward. But my mind was more focused on Melissa. I feared another delay, another ADA, another investigator. We had enough for an arrest warrant. There was enough reasonable suspicion, circumstantial evidence, and probable cause to arrest a month ago. We had now added a new witness along with corroborating testimony from the suspect's daughter.

I had one more idea to keep this case from taking another back seat. Nancy Grace was my prosecutor when I was assigned to the major case division with the Crime Commission. The entrance at 136 Pryor Street has three separate gold double doors that greet you as you walk into the Fulton County Courthouse. I've passed through those doors many times for a variety of reasons—court cases, task force meetings, and behind closed doors with judges. I used to love visiting Nancy's office. She always had some interesting case files or crime artifacts out. I remember once she had a sawed-off shotgun and a clock sitting on her desk. I knew there was a story there, and I couldn't wait to hear it.

I remembered one of those days in that courthouse where Nancy had a clergy member as part of her witness list. Nancy placed the preacher on the stand to testify about having been called to the defendant's jail cell.

Nancy's a smart cookie, and she knew better than anyone that she couldn't ask the preacher about their conversation. That conversation was off limits because it was protected as privileged. Instead, she quickly asked, "That whole time you were there with the defendant, did he ever ask you to pray for his dead wife?"

"No," the minister replied quickly. Then an avalanche of defense objections hit the courtroom. But the jury had heard it. The information was received loud and clear.

Nancy later said in an interview, "I saw this look of disbelief from these four ladies on the first row [of the jury box], I knew that was it. I had him."

Maybe this was the answer to our need to get the preacher on the stand in Melissa's case? Don't ask what Christopher talked to him about; ask him what Christopher did *not* talk to him about. I ran the questions over in my mind. "Did Christopher ask you to pray for Melissa to come back to him? Did he ask that you pray for her safety? Did he ask that you pray for their children? No more questions, Your Honor."

From May 30 to June 2, 2024, I was in Nashville, Tennessee, as a speaker for CrimeCon. To best explain what this event is, their website says it all:

> True Crime is so much more than murder, recreations and serial killers. This genre is rich with real-life stories of triumph and tragedy; heartbreak and heroism. It runs the gamut from the criminal mind to the criminal act, to the criminal justice system leaping into action. It's about psychology, victimology, and methodology. It covers seemingly unrelated disciplines as wide-ranging as science, art, and history and topics as diverse as domestic violence, fraud, stalking, coercive control, wrongful convictions, and more. It's always changing, evolving, and mirroring what is happening in society at large.

> And that is where CrimeCon comes in. From the latest cases to the latest advanced scientific techniques that help solve them. From the newest TV shows and docs to the best crime and mystery podcasts in the world. And from deep dives into topics you didn't even know existed to big ballroom sessions with personalities you watch or listen to every week—CrimeCon is the platform that brings the content, and the community, together.
>
> Our events are equal parts education and experience. We work hard to curate a wide-ranging program that has something for everyone and that combines hands-on learning with plenty of chances to interact with speakers, podcasters, and other members of the community.
>
> Despite that, hardly a day goes by that our team doesn't think about the fact that the things we cover often involve the worst day of someone's life. Respect for victims, families, and law enforcement is always at the forefront of everything we do, and we take this responsibility very seriously. We are proud to have introduced many families and victims to a passionate, empathetic community of people who want to help.
>
> We've been humbled by the reaction to CrimeCon since producing our first event in Indianapolis in 2017. Seeing the lives that have been changed as a result of this community coming together makes us all very proud to be a part of it.

I have had the good fortune to be a part of, work with, and meet some of the top experts, victims, and victims' families involved with CrimeCon since 2017. I haven't missed a CrimeCon yet and sho' Lord don't intend to. It's a career-enhancing, cold-case-igniting, and personally electrifying event. The people make the weekend. The CrimeCon staff are second to none. They somehow, with over 6,500 attendees, make certain that we have a personal touch on our sessions, booths, and meet and greets. The attendees and participants are outstanding people from all walks of life who come together to advocate, help solve a cold case, and offer support and friendship to victims, families of victims, and the experts working the case. I have showcased a cold case every year at CrimeCon, and I have had much success with cases getting national attention and civilians offering suggestions on how to solve a case, as well as victims receiving compassion, care, and financial assistance for testing of evidence.

The year 2024 was no different. I had thousands of people come to my sessions, drop by my table, or stop me in the halls. Hundreds asked about Melissa's case. They were invested from either our previous presentation at CrimeCon or the nine-part series we did on *Zone 7*. They wanted to know if the podcast had helped. Every single person asked me about Melissa's mom and sister. They asked about Melissa's children. I told them I prayed they felt a sense of pride knowing they stood up for their mother and made sure she was not lost in this investigation. They asked if I had met with Carl in person yet. I told them I had recently applied again to visit with him in person since he was moved and had a new warden. I said I hoped to hear soon after I returned home. They all understood the difference between interacting through letters versus sitting across from someone. I wished wardens felt the same way.

Chapter 33

HEAT WAVES AND BOILING POINTS

CARL BEING TRANSFERRED TO SAVANNAH wasn't good for anyone. But it did offer an opportunity. A new facility meant a new warden. I had mailed all the necessary paperwork, notarized, on May 7, 2024, and waited. I received an answer, postmarked May 24.

I sat and looked at the envelope before opening it. I felt like this was my last opportunity to visit with Carl face-to-face. We needed to hammer out our last-ditch efforts to see justice for Melissa. The fact the man had been hospitalized three times recently was a nagging thought I couldn't shake. Time was of the essence.

I opened the envelope and didn't need to read the whole letter. One word jumped out, loud and clear.

Denied.

Anger hit me hard and fast. How could people meet with serial killers like Dennis "BTK" Rader, Lawrence "the Toolbox Killer" Bittaker, and Wayne Williams and talk about their crimes? Carl and I were trying to solve the murder of his daughter! A cold case that had dragged on far, far too long.

The prison's response wasn't even professional. It was handwritten, one sentence at the top of the form that I had filled out. "Per Warden need to go through Metro for visit—Denied." No period, no comma, no subject. Carl Patton's visitor's request didn't even warrant a complete sentence.

I was seething. The hypocrisy of the "system" was maddening. There were media folks, writers, professors, and *fans* who had regular contact with killers. Just the previous day at CrimeCon, Lyle Menendez called in for a session! It was unjustified to me that Carl and I couldn't connect for a truly *innocent murder victim*. Yet all of these convicted killers could sell items, communicate with fans, and become the subjects of books, TV shows, and movies with access to the representatives at each medium, but Carl and I could not.

There was nothing else I could do but write another letter and wait two weeks for a reply.

On June 6, 2024, at 8:24 p.m., my phone rang. As per our signal, the next call came right at 8:25. Although I hurried, I couldn't catch it fast enough. My hands were filled with a string of lights. My sisters Sharlene and Sharon were putting the finishing touches around the house for Zoe's second baby shower, this one in Georgia. The yard was rich with the smell of early June and weddings. The gardenias were in bloom. The small, white, sweet-smelling flowers made me happy. When people ask me why I love them, I say because they *smell* like a wedding! My mother would say that in the South, "Every bride needs a gardenia in her bouquet." My momma couldn't be there for my wedding, but rest assured I had a gardenia or five in my bouquet.

Once I get free from the string of lights, I called the number back, reverse signaling that I was now free to talk. I allowed it to ring only twice in case a guard was making a round. I didn't leave a message because, again, I didn't want the phone to ping or illuminate. My phone rang right back, and I heard the familiar, "Ms. Sheryl, it's Carl Patton."

He sounded upbeat, and I could hear a friend of his in the background. The friend went silent, realizing that I'd answered, and then Carl spoke again. "Do you think we're closer?"

I told him, yes, we were closer. "I think we'll be done by July 4."

He said, "I heard Detective Shephard's on vacation till after the fourth."

I grinned, acknowledging to myself the prison information highway was alive and well. I assured Carl that even if Shephard was out of town, the DA's office was putting the finishing touches on the case file for the district attorney to review and approve for the grand jury.

Carl asked if the new witness who had come forward spoke with Shephard. I confirmed Shephard spoke with not only the new witness but with Christina, too. Both gave statements that were powerful additions to the case file.

I told him about sending an email to the DA's office detailing a way that would allow the preacher to testify. I explained how I remembered Nancy Grace's case when she called a clergyman to the stand. I told him how with carefully worded questions, we could get the answers we needed without breaking that protected privilege. We only needed to ask the preacher one question: Did Christopher tell you Melissa left for California?

Carl agreed on the question, then he slowly said, "Well, I hear you were denied permission to visit with me. Why?"

"I don't know. The paperwork didn't say. All it said was I needed to go through Metro."

"Metro? I'm not at Metro."

I told him the whole thing was baffling. It was just absurd. I told him if I heard anything I would try and get in touch with him. He said he hated where he was. He said they moved him for medical reasons and they hadn't even taken his blood pressure. The last thing he said before we hung up was, "Christopher needs to be in here. And I need to be home."

As I slipped the phone in my pocket, I listened to my sisters laughing in the background. I watched the lightning bugs dance around the lake flowers low to the ground at dusk and then higher in the pine trees as it got darker. Two of my favorite things happening in one of my favorite places. I often tell people my job has made me a better wife and mother. I take nothing for granted and I have no regrets. I love wide open and enjoy life furiously.

I looked around me, smiled, and took it all in because Carl couldn't, Melissa couldn't, and our mother couldn't.

I parked behind a small, white chapel to eat my lunch while enjoying a beautiful spring day. The sky was a perfect shade of blue, and the clouds were big and fluffy. I liked to come to this spot and sit and just watch the birds and squirrels, and of course, admire all the blooming flowers. The park that surrounded this sweet little church was quiet and shaded.

Although the serene surroundings were nearly perfect, I couldn't help but wonder why I hadn't received a reply to the email I'd sent the DA's office about the preacher. I sent it on June 6, 2024. The email detailed Nancy Grace's case she prosecuted and the way she used a preacher and his testimony without violating the privilege. Now it was June 13, 2024, and I hadn't heard anything from their office.

The pattern of no response was baffling and frustrating. I was reminded of all the cold case families I had worked with over the last twenty years. They all say the same thing, time and time again: "The police won't call me back, the detective won't respond to my voicemails, the prosecutor won't respond to my emails."

I am a working CSI. I am supposedly well respected on a national level. I have worked on cold cases with much success on a national level and have trained law enforcement around the world on investigative methods I developed. I served on the local DA's Cold Case Task Force, and I couldn't get a response. It was disrespectful at best.

Respond to victims. Respond to family members of victims. Respond to colleagues. It takes less time to respond than it does to read the email, listen to the voicemail, or take a call. Text! Send a fast, simple text: I got your message, nothing new to report but still working. Thank you again for reaching out.

Frankly, this is why victims, their families, and the public lose trust in an investigation or a detective. If they don't hear from you, they can't fully believe you are working for them. They have no proof you're doing anything.

For freak's sake—prove it to them. Call them back!

Day 1,042—at least that's what it felt like—and still no response. It was June 18, 2024 . I hadn't said anything to Carl or Norma, but the odds of the DA's office moving on this case before the Fourth of July were about a million to one. The courthouse would be all but empty the short week of the Fourth. That year the Fourth fell on a Thursday, and Friday was a given holiday. Most folks would take the whole week off because they only would have to burn two vacation days.

What made it so much worse was my belief that we were *so* close. I believed it in my heart. I felt it in my bones like a farmer can feel the rain. We were so damn close to a grand jury and an arrest.

I skipped the little white chapel and that day I was sitting at the picnic table at the back of the police station thinking about a text I'd received three years ago.

It was from Norma. It was the first text I'd received from her. June 14, 2021. In typical Norma fashion it was short, direct, and to the point: Call my cell!

We were scheduled to tape a segment on the local news with Karyn Greer the next day. In that same vein, I got another text from Norma on the fifteenth: Just talked to 20/20.

No fanfare, no excitement, no fan girling, but just the facts. Norma had had some health issues during our time on Melissa's case. She was in the hospital in October of 2021. She struggled some and would call me between breathing treatments.

One of her "not so like her" texts came on November 12, 2021. She said: You are the most awesome person I have ever met and so thankful for your help on Melissa's case.

But that was then and this was now. I didn't deserve it then, and I didn't deserve it now. It had taken all this time, and we were still not at the finish line. And Christopher was still walking around free. That hurt most of all.

As I sat there in the hot Georgia heat, my frustration was growing. The inaction and stalls this case had seen were pushing me to a boiling point. I wanted to call the DA's office and tell them all that their lack of action was straight up an injustice to this family. It made me wonder if it had anything to do with the Patton family's background. It shouldn't have, and it would be criminal if it did.

But as I sat and daydreamed about cussing folks out, I saw the trash dumpster to my right. It was filled with large black trash bags. I could see five bags. And then suddenly out of nowhere was a beautiful butterfly. I watched her fly around the bags, landing only for a moment on one of them, and then she was gone.

Okay, I got it. I felt it. I was not going to ignore the obvious metaphor. I would choose to concentrate on all the good work we had done, while also processing the setbacks we encountered.

* December 15, 2021, we found the trash bags. They were all still intact with the knots in place. I called just in time to stop the evidence from going to the state lab. We were able to get all the bags to a private lab with renowned experts.

* We got CrimeCon 2023 in Orlando, Florida, to allow us to present Melissa's case. When Norma Patton went on stage, it was the first time a convicted "killer" was onstage.

* August 18, 2022, I reached out to Norma because I had not been able to reach Tina in a while. Norma texted back in classic Norma style: She's in jail, violation of probation.

* There was another witness who wrote to the parole board on Carl's behalf. Her name was Elaine. She was sexually abused by one of Carl's victims, and her daughter, Stephanie, wrote the board and thanked Carl for saving her mother more abuse.

* December 30, 2022, we started the *Zone 7* podcast on the Flint River Killer's daughter's murder. We had hoped it would compel someone to come forward. We knew now that it did.

* January 2, 2023, Carl called to say he saw me on Fox News and finally knew what I looked like. This was a strange call for me, because I had not thought about Carl not knowing me or what I looked like. I knew so much about him: what he looked like, his family, his crimes, his homes, his children, his company, his prison records, his health concerns, his marriage. This list goes on.

* February 15, 2023, a text from Norma: They got DNA sample from Chris.

* March 13, 2023, one of the gifts of any cold case investigation is being able to talk to the first detective on the case. There are always going to be facts, beliefs, theories, and gut feelings that never make the police reports. It was such a gift when I had the opportunity to speak with Detective Alton Calhoun. He also agreed to come on *Zone 7* to help promote someone coming forward with information about who might have killed Melissa.

* April 20, 2023, Norma texted me: Stein feels the bag DNA wasn't good enough. Damn. I was hoping the DNA somehow was preserved in the elements all those years.

* June 13, 2023, text from Norma reads: Grand Jury subpoenas being worked on. Well, that never happened. More waiting. More wondering what was happening. This kind of behavior didn't fly. On top of actions like the mother and sister of the suspect flat-out ignored subpoenas and just didn't show up? I know I'd be in jail if I did that. Why were they treated differently? Why were they allowed to tell the court that they had a new job and couldn't miss work and didn't drive in traffic? Hello? What the hell? Call Uber! The first line of any subpoena states, "Laying All Other Business Aside." This was absolutely maddening. These two individuals, in my opinion, absolutely had information as to what happened to Melissa. His momma wouldn't have dragged him to see the preacher if she didn't suspect

what he'd done. His sister wouldn't have busted out crying at Lowe's if she didn't suspect what he had done.

* July 11, 2023, the grand jury was postponed for the Trump investigation.

* October 24, 2023, the DA's office told the family to expect the grand jury now to be in November.

* December 4, 2023, text from Norma: They're not answering phone or emails.

* December 19, 2023, DA's office completed interviews with mother and sister of Christopher Wolfenbarger.

* January 23, 2024, Detective Shephard told me he was ready to get a warrant. Did Christopher ever file for divorce? He told Calhoun he did. Christopher told Detective Calhoun he saw Melissa in the spring of 1999. It's hard to know what the truth is when statements change. Did Melissa just leave? Did Christopher drop her off at a train station? Did they go and eat fast food? One would think the last time you saw the love of your life, the mother of your children, you would remember what you said and did.

* April 29, 2024, text from Norma: 25 years ago her head was found and 21 since I buried her. A hard day for me. Norma told me once, "My family is smaller now, but I'll make it through." She once had Melissa to love, a son-in-law to rely on, grandchildren to spoil, and a husband to share it all with. When she lost Melissa, she lost more than her daughter. She lost everything.

Chapter 34

CLEANING THE BARN

ON JUNE 20, 2024, I received an email reminder that the Cold Case Task Force was still meeting today. The sender apologized for the last-minute notice, 9:40 a.m., but also said the meeting was still set for 10:00 a.m. at the Roswell Police Department. That department was forty-five minutes away from me in traffic. I wrote back and asked if there was an update. The sender replied that the DDA would be the one to update us. Good thing I didn't hold my breath.

Four days later, it's a Monday. And it's 97 degrees. No matter how much I willed the phone to ring or my email indicator to ding, time didn't stand still for waiting. Life moved on, crime still happened, and I was called out on other cases.

I would have loved to hunker down in the evidence room where it was cool. The cement walls help trap the coolness that make the cinder blocks cool to the touch. But, as it was, another case had just come in. When I opened the door to my CSI truck, it felt like I was opening the oven checking on biscuits. It was only the third week of June. We had at least eleven weeks of this spa treatment left.

As I looked for shade to park my all-black vehicle while I helped search for a missing person, I thought of Melissa. She had been missing for so long, and Carl and Norma had to do most of the searching all on their own.

Still no word from the DA's office. No returned email, phone call, or note regarding where we stood with the case. I texted Norma, and she hadn't heard anything either. She said she'd asked for updates but so far, she hadn't heard a word. Detective Shephard wouldn't return from vacation until next week. I'd call him then and tell him the idea that Nancy Grace used with the preacher.

At least there was some good news that came out of the day—the missing person returned home! Thank goodness for small miracles.

That whole week, I honestly felt like I was melting. The Georgia heat wave was relentless. I was working an armed robbery with no air-conditioning in the store. Part of me thought these guys were going to get away with this because I couldn't stay in this devil's-bedroom-level heat searching for evidence. I took breaks and gathered all the evidence left behind.

I was feeling some relief seated in my truck with the air-conditioning blowing full blast in my face. My phone pinged and it was Norma with a text message. It was a screenshot of a text message from DDA Faucette: Good Afternoon. We are still on our same timeline to meet with our unit head about our recommendation. That will happen this week or next week. I will know more about a timeline to meet with the district attorney after the initial one.

The message came through to me on June 26, 2024, at 2:00 p.m. A Wednesday. A Wednesday *afternoon*, at that. Let's be honest. Everyone who has ever worked for a city government agency knows how likely it is that on a Wednesday afternoon at 2:00 p.m., if you don't already have a meeting set with a supervisor for Thursday or Friday, it ain't happening that week. We all know at the *earliest* it'll be sometime next week. Why don't they just tell her the truth? Tell her they were ready to go forward but had to run it past the powers that be, and that could take at least two weeks. Norma's waited over thirty years. I figured she could handle another month.

It wasn't lost on me that the screenshotted text Norma had sent me had been a reply to hers. Once again, the burden of communication rested with the victim's family. I hope young officers, detectives, prosecutors, CSIs, chiefs, and sheriffs will understand how much families are desperate for any morsel of information. They crave contact with "their" detective or prosecutor. There's even a program that allows you to call someone and bypass their phone ringing. The call goes straight to voicemail. You can call a victim, family of a victim, task force members, whomever and simply leave a message without having to talk to them.

When I was with the Crime Commission and an investigator with juvenile court in Cobb County, I set aside a day a month to call victims all day long with updates, checking in, or just touching base. Most often there was no update of a court date, restitution, witnesses coming forward, evidence testing back, or plea deals. But it was imperative that they heard from me. It was equally important for me to hear them talk about anniversary dates, birthdays, holidays missed, people they suspected, rumors they may have heard, fears, frustrations, and very often appreciation. Most calls took less than sixty seconds: "Hello __________, there's no news. I just wanted you to know I was thinking about you and __________. I wanted you to know we are still working and trying to develop more leads. Please call me if you hear anything. You might think of something or hear from someone before we do."

It's July 4, 2024, and I texted Norma to check on Carl. I hadn't received a letter or a call recently. I wanted to be sure he was doing well health-wise.

Norma texted: It's really hard for him. The hardest time he has had. The Warden cut out the food at visitation. Inmate gets a bottle of water and a bag of chips, that's it.

The waiting was getting harder for everyone. This case was in the hands of others to act on. It was their timetable, their move, and their call. However, one thing I try to teach rookies is there's no holding pattern in investigations. The work never stops. Today, I was going to write Carl and call Norma. I'd ask: Have we forgotten anyone: a teacher, dance coach, probation officer, anyone we need to have interviewed? You never know what will be the coup de grace or the clincher for a juror.

The Karen Read trial is a perfect example. Ms. Read was on trial for murder. There were two camps: She did it and she didn't do it. There was nobody in the middle of the road. Big divide and serious debates online. Her first trial ended in a hung jury. Everyone lists different reasons why they still think she killed her boyfriend, John O'Keefe, while others list reasons why they still think she didn't do it. All the witnesses, evidence, experts, and people are still dug into their camps. There will have to be "new" evidence, witnesses, or experts in order for anyone to possibly consider changing their mind on this case. Maybe, on Melissa's case we could find one more friend she'd confided in, a coworker who witnessed abuse, a court reporter who heard her admit the violence she'd experienced at the hands of her husband. The additional evidence could be the clincher!

I was moving forward. I would not rest until this case was closed. Trying means failed. The opposite of trying is doing. I was going to be doing! I would do this investigation till it was done! Through all the inactivity, stalls, new detectives, new DA, new ADAs, we had been working, and we were not going to stop now.

My mother and I were traveling through the Amish country about thirty-five years ago. We stopped and had the opportunity to speak with a family selling bread and pies on the side of a two-lane road outside of Lancaster, Pennsylvania. The young father was tending to the horse and carriage, and my mother asked him if he worked in the fields everyday tending to his crops. He smiled at her and said, "Unless it's raining."

My mother laughed and said, "What do you do if it's raining?"

He replied, "That's God telling me to clean the barn."

There are many times on a cold case when you must "clean the barn."

I don't trust people's words. I'll even question their actions. But patterns are 100 percent my barometer. Nancy Grace always says, "If you want to know about a horse, look at his track record."

Well, I say if you want to know about a POS, look at his rap sheet! There was a young woman killed by an ex-boyfriend who beat her. Went to jail. Was given a high bond. Dad told the judge if the ex gets out, he will kill her. Judge lowers bond. No ankle monitor. No victim notification. Subject makes bond. Kills her.

Looking at the pattern of their relationship, it was all too familiar: He beat her, she'd leave, police and family would help her, he would convince her to come back to him. He'd beat her she'd leave, police and family would help her, he would convince her to come back to him. The pattern! The pattern! The pattern! Melissa and Christopher had a clear and present pattern! Don't believe words, don't believe actions, believe patterns! Why did this pattern break? Why this last time did Christopher not convince her to come back to him? Why did she not return to him? In the police report written by Detective AB Calhoun, Christopher told him he last saw Melissa "walking down the street towards the house. He said he picked her up and they drove to Taco Bell and they talked about their relationship. He then dropped her off at the train station." According to the police report Christopher originally told Calhoun he would take a voice stress test but declined when the test was about to begin. Questions, if you are paying attention, are statements. The person asking might be trying to be slick. Pay attention—they'll tell on themselves. Watch an old episode of *Perry Mason* for proof. My family loved that show. My parents and sisters, even our grandparents, liked the courtroom crime drama. Mason was a defense attorney who won almost all his cases. Often by listening to what wasn't said just as much as what was. My sister Sharlene and I never missed an episode of *Perry Mason* when we were younger.

When two prisoners are separated, they know they each can gain important benefits from cooperating or suffer from failing to do so but find it difficult to coordinate their stories. This can be applied to any situation in which two entities are trying to figure out what benefits them. In the prisoner's dilemma, it's either working with police to get a deal or keeping their mouth shut and not risking being harmed or ostracized by becoming a snitch. It's an inmate's catch-22.

Carl understood this dilemma. He lived it and watched it most days. He had to decide when he first reached out to a detective to help find Melissa. He had to come to terms again when he appeared on my podcast and showed real remorse, feelings, and sorrow. These feelings can be seen as weakness in his world.

Carl also had the two-edged sword of us utilizing the media. I explained to him that the media is an invaluable tool in cold cases. It gets the attention of law enforcement, district attorneys, potential witnesses, and the victim's family and most importantly sends a message to the killer. Carl had to be careful participating in media stories and the podcast through his letters because if the prison knew he had access to cell phones, he could get in big trouble.

I was hesitant to bring it up at the time except to show Carl was who he had always been. He'd stop at nothing to get to the end of this road. The prisoner's dilemma would not stop Carl. In many ways it fueled him. It was the ultimate game inside the walls of his prison. He knew he was old school and smarter than most guards and young punk inmates. They didn't know the game. I knew that Carl was waiting for the day Christopher was headed to a prison cell. I knew that he secretly hoped Christopher would live the dilemma, too.

Chapter 35

THE CALL

THE FOURTH OF JULY CAME and went. On July 8, Norma texted me: Haven't heard from anyone yet.

We were getting down to the wire with this case. One way or the other we'd reached the time to fish or cut bait. Melissa deserved a day in court. She deserved for her children to hear that she didn't abandon them. To hear from their aunt and grandmother that she would have never left them. Frankly, her children deserved that, too. Norma went on to text, Officials are still not giving us a date, same ole same ole. Really getting frustrated.

July 15, 2024, another text from Norma: Carl has been in hospital again. Fluid buildup.

The Cold Case Task Force had a Zoom meeting that week. I hoped we'd get an update on Melissa's case. I knew there were others on the task force who were interested in it. Plus, I had some real concerns about Carl's health. I wanted him to have some good news soon.

On July 23, the Cold Case Task Force with the DA's office met over Zoom. They updated Melissa's case. The case packet had been cleared to go to District Attorney Fani Willis for final approval for indictment. DDA Faucette said he believed the case would get indicted within thirty days. I updated the group on Carl's health issues. They were aware that Norma had surgery set for next week. It was considered minor, but heath issues can be tricky.

For the first time in a long while, I felt good about Melissa's case.

A few days later, it was pouring down rain and I was parked in my squad car in the cemetery. The rain was coming down so hard everything was blurred. I had gotten a letter from Carl, and this quiet, historical place seemed like a nice place to sit and read while I ate my lunch.

Carl wrote that he had an idea that he wanted me to present to the ADA once Christopher was arrested and given a public defender. He said that a plea bargain might be discussed, and he wanted as part of the deal for Christopher to tell where Melissa's torso was so they could "bring all of her home." How ironic that I was sitting in a cemetery right down the street from Waffle House where Melissa worked, and just a few miles from where her other remains were found.

Walt woke me up sweetly at 6:30 a.m. I was catching a flight that morning headed to Arizona. I was excited to see part of Arizona I'd never seen before. I was headed to Show Low, where I'd be training the Apache Nation Police on recovery of human remains. It was an honor to teach with the Cold Case Foundation for the Bureau of Indian Affairs. This adventure was the only reason I was halfway okay leaving my family. Both Huck and Caroline were home visiting, and I hated leaving them even for three days. I had been away from Walt only a handful of times since we got married. I preferred to travel with him or the kids or one of my sisters.

But this one time, I'd man up, so to speak, and go have a tremendous time meeting incredible people and seeing amazing places. I'd miss my family, but I'd bring them some pretty cool gifts.

Walt was driving with one hand while holding my hand with the other. He knew I hated to be without him. This was a spectacular opportunity and would be a great experience. It would have been perfect if he or the kids could come. I would have loved for them to see these sights, too.

Walt was pulling off the highway into the airport when my phone rang. It was 9:38 a.m., and it was Norma calling. I had a gut feeling this was the call.

I grab the phone. "Hello," I said as fast as I could because I didn't want to delay the news.

"He's in custody! He's in custody!" Norma was crying and laughing at the same time.

I was nearly doing the same. "Really?" I was fighting to hold back tons of emotions.

"I wouldn't kid you about this!"

"How did you find out?"

Norma said that Detective Shephard had just called her. She called Christina first, then me. I got chocked up at that—this had been quite the investigation.

I asked her when she was going to be able to tell Carl. He needed to know. He deserved to know.

Norma said he was set to call on Thursday. I hated he'd be the last to know unless it made the news. As much as the media had helped us, it didn't seem right for him to hear it that way.

I didn't have to worry long. Calhoun, the original investigator on Melissa's case, made a call to a higher-up to have him tell Carl. What a thoughtful and kind thing for him to do for Carl. Father to father. He knew that Carl deserved to know that the man, the coward, who had butchered his baby girl had finally been arrested.

Monday, and I was back at work from an incredible trip out to Arizona. Training the Apache Rangers in recovery of human remains was beyond amazing, but it didn't measure up to knowing Christopher Wolfenbarger had been arrested.

My phone pinged with a text message. It was Tina. Morning at the doctor's with Mom she wants to see you!

I was thrilled to see them after such incredible news and told them to come by the station when they were finished at the doctor. I hated that I was out of town for the press conference. I wanted to stand with them literally and figurately.

Twenty minutes later I had a new text message: Here!

As I walked to the lobby of the police department, I was filled with joy in anticipation of seeing and hugging them. This had been a long, hard road.

For me it had been seven years of roadblocks, stalls, and downright ignoring this case. And right now, it had all been worth it. Right now, knowing Christopher Wolfenbarger was sitting in Rice Street was a victory.

I opened the door and saw Norma sitting in one of the old gray steel chairs that had hosted many a criminal, victim, and expert visitor alike. She saw me and stood up with more energy than I'd seen her have in years. She looked ten years younger. Her hair, skin, and walk were younger. We hugged. She cried. Then Tina grabbed me and we hugged. It was an overdue moment.

After a good, long visit where we laughed, cried, and laughed some more, we took a selfie in my office. I couldn't get over the change in Norma. She glowed with pure happiness. And Tina looked focused. Like she had future goals because this case wasn't holding her in place any longer. She hadn't been able to move on from it. She had to see this through for Melissa, for her momma, for her dad. Now for the first time in twenty-five years, she could plan her next steps free of this burden.

In the spirit of what *Zone 7* is, Dr. Angie Arnold and her husband, John, hosted a dinner for the family and experts who worked on Melissa's case. Dr. Arnold has been a steadfast and compassionate part of this team of brilliant and devoted people. I had called Angie and told her I was looking at a couple of places to hold a Case Closed Ceremonial Dinner, and she didn't hesitate. "Please let John and I do this," she said. "We want to. It would mean so much for us to do this, and you know this is our way of giving back."

Giving back? I told her she was crazy. All she does is give back. She has traveled, spoken, provided expert profiles, hosted events, and answered calls whenever I have needed her. She has never asked for a dime.

For the celebration, the Arnolds reserved the 1912 Room at the Ansley Golf Club in a posh part of Atlanta. She told me the room was the prettiest one the club had, and it held up to forty guests. "Please invite all the experts," she said.

Forty! What a generous gift. Dinner at the club for forty people? What a night it would be. The guest list was legendary. Each expert was among the best in the country.

Once you take two steps inside the lobby of the golf club, you see a grand piano, flower arrangements worthy of a royal wedding, and marble floors that shine under the chandeliers. The 1912 Room had a bank of windows across the back of the room overlooking the pool. With the night sky we could see the Atlanta skyline, the sunset, and the lit pool. It was a stunning site. Each table had a candle glowing, full place setting, with double tablecloths and fancy chairs. We had a specialty drink and a Mardi Gras–influenced menu.

After dinner there were a few speeches. I needed to thank everyone for giving their time and offering hope and support to the family.

Then Norma's cell phone rang, and it was Carl. He wanted to call and thank everyone at the event personally. He spoke with Norma and Tina first. Then Norma gave the phone to Karyn Greer. Carl said he was appreciative of all her coverage and for keeping Melissa's case alive for twenty years. He then told Nancy Grace that no one else could have taken this case nationally like she did. He was grateful for CrimeCon, *Crime Stories with Nancy Grace*, and CrimeOnLine, but mostly he was grateful for her compassion. Carl told them I was the one who got them all there and got this case done. He then stated again, just 'cause the case was solved for me not to go anywhere. I assured him I was not going away.

And then he asked to speak to Detective Shephard. It was a powerful moment for me watching this detective speak with the father of a murder victim, but yet a killer himself. Detective Shephard was kind and respectful. He accepted the thank-you with grace and charity. This moment hit extra hard for me because the original detective on the case, Detective Calhoun, was set to join us, but he texted me earlier and said his mother died suddenly and he was on his way out of town to be with family. I wanted Calhoun to have that moment where Carl could tell him how much his actions had meant to him. But Calhoun was once again taking care of a family—this time his own.

That night, when the celebrating was done, I still had more to say. When the call finally came—Christopher Wolfenbarger was arrested for the murder of Melissa Wolfenbarger—I was thinking of Carl, Norma, and Tina. After all the trials, roadblocks, stalls, and some folks just not giving a damn—finally, justice for Melissa. My heart broke for her children. In the most raw and real of ways, they had lost both parents. I was sorry that they would now have to face a trial, facts, and results from a jury. As I was told so many years ago from a man that I love and admire, a friend and mentor, Chief Eddie Moody: "Sometimes you never know what happened, and sometimes you know exactly what happened. Both are difficult and gut wrenching."

Melissa, I'm sorry. I'm sorry this happened to you. I'm sorry it took so long. I'm just sorry for all of it. Justice is a difficult concept for me, because there's no way to truly receive it. There's nothing we can take from Christopher that equals what was taken from Norma. Christopher will lose his freedom, but he is alive, his children are alive. There's no "justice." The eye for an eye doesn't exist. No one wins in murder; there is only loss.

There have been many God Grin'n moments in my life. A grin is to me a smile with an acknowledgment of understanding with humor. You grin when you know your son is mischievous but still cute and funny. You grin when you realize your husband is giving you that romantical signal. You grin when you realize your sister hates the same person you do. When you see your daughter's grin after her sarcastic humor, and you know where she gets it. Therefore, a God Grin'n moment is when the Good Lord above sees you as the less than perfect, trying to do good soul and still as the all-seeing higher power that gives you a grin every now and then. Just a quick half smile, acknowledgment that you done good, or you tried, or I'm just gonna give you this one.

God has grinned all over this case for me. Given many gifts. Shown his grace and love. Even with these horrible crimes, his light was there. You could see it. It was there when Nancy Grace stepped forward to bring attention to this case as she and only she could do. When Angie Arnold said, "I'm gonna call and check on Tina." When Duanne Thompson drove hours to work a metal detector in the Georgia heat to search for a saw in the woods. When Trace Sargent used her sensational dogs to search for Melissa's torso. When Karyn Greer saw the momma, not a case or a story. When Carl Patton called and got choked up telling you he listened to Liddie Evans's children on your podcast and he now knew what he did to them. Because of the pain and heartbreak over Melissa's murder and what he felt. He knew and he was sorry. When Carl Patton after twenty-five years asked you to tell Liddie's children was he sorry, God was grinning.

Chapter 36

PLEA DEALS, BOND HEARINGS, AND JURY DUTY?

CHRISTOPHER WOLFENBARGER WAS SET TO appear in court for a plea hearing. I kept remembering what Carl had specified: The family could accept a plea deal *if* Christopher revealed where he disposed of the rest of Melissa's body. Although the family had long ago buried what little they had, Carl wanted her whole again.

Would Christopher agree to it? I wanted to believe he would. I wanted to believe he had at least one molecule of human decency in his being, but I had my doubts. Besides, who's to say he wouldn't send us on a wild-goose chase in search of something he knew wasn't there?

It turned out, today wasn't the day we'd find out. The hearing was postponed. I'd sworn I wouldn't get angry again with the system over all the delays this case had already seen. But it was hard. Families gear up for each court date. The emotions of the murder, the cold case, the arrest, and everything in between over the last two and a half decades was boiling up. They were going to come face-to-face with the accused killer for the first time in years. They might run into his family in the halls of the courthouse. Tensions run high with everyone on edge.

Then there's the logistics. They had to decide who's driving, where to park, do they have change for the meters? It may seem silly, but even what to wear is a decision they had to make. Used to be, there was a certain protocol for court hearings. You weren't expected to wear your Sunday best, but a certain amount of decorum was expected.

Then it's all for naught. The proceeding's postponed. No reason, no heads-up—just it's not going to happen today.

I'd been around the business enough to know it could possibly take weeks, *several* weeks, to get it back on the court calendar.

Two steps forward, one step back. But no need to get frustrated. We had the arrest.

~

My phone pinged with a text from Norma. I read the first line and fell out laughing. The darkest cases and the worst of times, you can sometimes still find humor. Laughter is a gift, some even say medicine. I was getting a good dose that morning.

Norma had been summoned for jury duty! She texted further: I think they'll cancel because of my concealment charge.

She was probably right about that!

She continued: These questions should get me excluded and removed from the list. She sent me screenshots of the questions: "Have you or a family member ever had a particularly positive or negative experience with the court system?"

By now, I'm crying laughing and texted back, Don't forget Fayette.

She texted question number 2: "Have you or someone close to you ever been a victim of a crime?"

I texted: Well, that one got me—sad.

Norma replied: No can't laugh at that one.

But to make certain we ended on a laughing note, she texted question number 3: Have you or a family member ever tried to have someone arrested? She asked: Is this a yes or no?

I had to call her! We laughed until we cried—it was good to hear her laugh. The next morning, I got a follow-up text: I'm excused from jury duty!

Well, that was definitely the right call.

At Christopher's first bond hearing, he showed up in a wheelchair. The defense attorney said that Melissa's mother and sister couldn't be afraid of his client. His reasoning? They'd done the podcast *Zone 7*. Did that mean my podcast had new followers? I suppressed a slight grin. The attorney asked if they were so afraid of Christopher, why would they do any media at all?

Tina was a little worried that the judge might agree that because Christopher had not had any major arrests in twenty-five years, he'd grant the $25,000 bond the defense was asking for. The judge didn't go for it. No bond was appropriate due to the amount of time and the brutality of the murder.

To me, it was quite telling that Christopher's mother didn't make a plea for his release.

After the hearing, Tina and Norma met me for lunch. We talked about the hearing, next steps in the process, Carl's health, Christopher in the wheelchair, his son Alias, his attempt to stare Tina down, and when we thought the trial might start. It was nice to just chat about the case without the sense of urgency and frustration.

Back at the office, the odds and ends and bits and pieces of scattered information were slowly coming together. Norma texted me and asked that I call her.

Once we got on the phone, she said she found online where Christopher Wolfenbarger did a quitclaim, deed transfer, to his girlfriend, Kara Samples. The same live-in girlfriend who on police body cam lied to the police by telling them Christopher was not at home. The body cam footage went on to show Christopher hiding behind a wine rack.

This quitclaim was done on June 7, 2023. I found that extremely interesting timing. When the Atlanta Police were contacting his mother and sister and scheduling a time to reinterview them, the DA's office was working hard getting subpoenas typed up and signed. Christopher was clearly concerned about the police activity.

I went back and checked a message I had received over social media from Christopher's son, Joey. It was dated June 11, 2023, at 9:34 p.m.: I've been listening to the interviews regarding Melissa Wolfenbarger…she was my mother and her side of the family is very shady.

I replied, asking him if he would like to tell his side of the story. I also told him how sorry I was for the loss of his mother. I told him to let me know if he wanted to talk. He went on to say, For everything you can find about the case it's only under her parent's point of view. I would agree to talk but to have my father present as well. I don't have any memories due to being 2yrs old at the time, but I've heard of things my family has said thru the years.

I told him I understood and again I was sorry about his mom. I added that he could let me know anytime if they wanted to talk.

Joey then said, "I appreciate it. I'll talk to him tomorrow. Would be coming to your office or you come to us?"

I told him either would work and it was his call. I never heard from him again.

Chapter 37

HE'S GONE

NINE DAYS BEFORE CHRISTMAS OF 2024, at 10:00 a.m. on the dot, Norma called. She was crying. She sobbed, "The prison just called. Carl's gone, he's dead."

I sat there, stunned. Norma's cell phone started ringing, so I told her I would call her back in about thirty minutes. As I hung up, I remembered she was the only person I knew who still had a home landline phone. She kept it for Carl to call on.

I called Tina because I knew she was driving to her mom's house. She answered the phone crying. Like her mother, she sobbed. "Not my dad, Sheryl. Not my dad!"

I didn't say anything, just giving her the moment to weep.

She finally asked, "How am I going to do this?"

I told her she was Carl Patton's daughter. That's how!

I called Detective Shephard. He is such a kind and devoted investigator. He thanked me for letting him know and said he was going to call Norma as soon as we hung up. I told him the thing that will give the family the most peace is knowing Christopher was arrested. I told him that he did that. He gave Carl that final chapter of his fight. If Carl had not seen Christopher arrested, I didn't believe the family would ever recover.

I called Norma back as promised. She had talked to the warden and was told the state would pay all funeral expenses. But there was a catch. Carl would be buried in a pauper's grave at the prison.

Norma said, "I just can't have him there forever. He needs to finally come home."

The warden told her if they didn't want the state to bury him, the expense of the funeral would be on her.

His official time of death was 9:41 a.m. I told her the idea that he was alone week after week in the hospital and she wasn't allowed to visit—not once? *That* was cruel and unusual punishment for them both.

I texted the experts, police, and media friends with the news. Dr. Angie Arnold called Tina immediately and offered her support.

Then Dr. Angie called me. She said, "I'm here for her. But I have to say I am a little shaken. But this goes to show you that as an inmate they don't care about you at all."

But some people do care. A lot.

Tina has worked at the same diner for years. Her regular customers like Al and Mike know her and she knows them. Al, who Tina calls Al-E-Gator, was one of her regulars. She knew right where he was gonna sit, what he wanted to eat, and the jokes he was gonna tell. You could count on the time and day Al was going to come by and have a meal and enjoy some conversation. Suddenly Al stopped coming by. Tina was concerned because he never missed a week without telling her he was going out of town or something.

A few days after Carl's death, Tina called me close to midnight and told me a Christmas miracle story. They didn't have $15,000 for a funeral for Carl, so they had opted to have him cremated for $3,500. They didn't have that amount of money, either, but they figured they might be able to raise it.

Carl and Norma's granddaughter started a GoFundMe. That raised a little over one hundred dollars. That Friday, a beautiful blonde woman walked into the diner. It was Mike's daughter. She told Tina that her father had died. She wanted to meet Tina, see her dad's booth, order his meal, and hear stories about him.

Tina cried as she told stories about Mike. Then she told the beautiful blonde that she had just lost her dad, too. It was a crazy sad bond they were sharing. Tina told her that the prison offered to bury him for free, but they would never leave him in prison forever.

The two women hugged goodbye and Tina felt an added sadness. She would miss Mike, and she felt empty inside missing her dad. Tina turned back to her other customers and made her way halfway through her shift. Her phone rang suddenly, and it was the funeral home. She didn't know why they were calling. They had made it clear they wouldn't do any of the work on her dad until they were paid in full. Tina answered anyway, still sad about Mike, her dad, and the situation.

The voice on the other end said, "I just wanted to call and tell you we have received $2,000 towards the services."

Stunned, Tina said, "What do you mean? How?"

The funeral home director said a beautiful blonde woman just came in and paid $2,000 for Carl's service. Tina stood silent. The overwhelming shock of the kindness was too much. The thoughtfulness of a stranger who was hurting and grieving, too.

Tina said to me, "Can you believe that? It's a miracle, a Christmas miracle!"

~

It was February 25, and as I parked my car on the street at Central Avenue near the corner of Mitchell Street, the memories came back, always vivid. The shooting. That day in March when we lost three of our own. A judge, court reporter, and a sheriff's deputy. I never walk into the Fulton County Court Building and not think about Judge Barnes, Julie, and Hoyt.

That day was no different. Their portraits hang in the lobby, and I found myself looking for them as soon as I passed the security area. My intern, Amena, came along with me today. It was always nice to have a new audience for my stories. She was about to get a tour, honey!

As we made our way to the fourth floor, a ton of memories came to me. I told Amena about Nancy Grace and Jim Burch, and about such well-known figures in the state court system as Shawn LaGrua, Lewis Slaton,

Sheila Ross, and Clint Rucker. I told her about my time with the Fulton County Sheriff's Office and the Jamil Abdullah al-Amin trial. We sat on the familiar wooden benches and heard attorneys talking about cases and trying to make a deal. Both sides want a "win," so they both benefit if they can agree on a plea deal.

I have never met or seen Christopher Wolfenbarger's defense attorney, but I spotted a man outside the courtroom waiting and laughingly told Amena, "I bet that's Chris's POS attorney."

I was right. Today was a motions hearing for Christopher Wolfenbarger. The defense wanted the case dismissed outright and made a motion to compel for the prosecution to present all evidence.

One of the motions was to quash the witness who came forward because of *Zone 7*. The prosecution stated they gave the witness's name to the defense already. It is amazing to me after all these years and all the cases and all the trials that there is still so much time wasted. Justice is not fast on either side.

Tina arrived and we passed the time talking and sharing stories. She shared two I had never heard in our seven years together. She said she guessed sitting outside of the court made her think of them.

"Okay, so what happened was I was sent to prison for VOP for two years. When I came home after doing a year and had parole, I went to see dad at Macon State while on parole no problem at all. Get off parole early, and 'bout six months later, Clayton County calls and threatens to lock me up for VOP again. I had to do five years' probation because they didn't have both probations on my paperwork. Asked PO if it was okay to visit Dad. They said yes, but when I went, Macon State pulled me out of visitation before Dad walks in, saying I can't 'cause I'm on probation. I raised hell, but it didn't do any good. I called Mom on my way back home. Dad had called to tell Mom, and he was raising hell. I talked to a few people, and no one could understand why. I called my friend who worked at the governor's mansion to get him to help. He called Macon State, and no luck getting the warden to agree with me seeing Dad. Next thing we know they shipped him to Dodge. Did paperwork for Dodge State and went to visit no problem and was still on probation. Wrote letters to DOC and parole board, and no one could help with Macon State. But because someone from the governor's office called Macon, they moved him farther away."

I had no idea that she had been kept away from her dad because of her criminal history. I knew of course that she had a criminal history, but I did not know it stopped her from visiting her father. I mean John Gotti Jr. got to visit his father, the Mafia don John Gotti! And for the record, I am all for that. I believe families should be able to visit, crime families or not.

Then in typical Tina fashion she dropped a bombshell. "Well yeah, that was pitiful, but it was not as crazy as when I wore a wire."

What? When? Where? She just said it like it was one of the most interesting statements she had ever made. Girl, come on now—you can't leave me in the dark! I've only worn a wire once—I had to know her circumstances.

Tina laughed a deep, raspy laugh and said, "You really want to know?" She smiled and said, "In 2003 we met with Calhoun downtown and were talking 'bout things to do. He asked if one of us would wear a wire to talk to a potential witness. I told him I would. So he got me dressed with a wire and Mom and I drove to Brookline and Calhoun in another car parked somewhere and listened."

Learn something new every day.

Today was the last chance for a plea deal to be entered prior to going to trial. And I heard that unmistakable sound of a flat tire. *Are you freaking kidding me?* Well, I was gonna miss court.

Sweet Walt came and tried to pump the tire up, but it wouldn't hold more than nine pounds of air. Yep, there was a hole in it. I told Walt to go on to work. He had a big meeting, and there was no reason to miss it. He insisted he would go home, change clothes, and come back. I told him I got paid by the hour, and I was fine standing right there until our friends at Parkers Towing sent help.

We kissed bye and said this was one of those stolen moments. We were grateful for a little extra time together. As I stood out beside my CSI truck waiting on the tow truck driver to come and help me, I was thankful for the nice cool breeze. It was almost cold. The sky was a beautiful pink- and red-streaked burst of color. The Canada geese were flying overhead. Fog was lifting off the lake. Our neighbor Ms. Timpy drove by and we talked. My new neighbor was walking her newest rescue puppy that I got to meet and love on him. And I thought what a sweet surprise to be able to enjoy all this. I wasn't stranded. I was given a gift!

I finally made it to the police station rolling in on my spare. Tina texted me they were leaving the courthouse. Before I could call her, Norma texted a two-word statement.

"Dwarf House!"

I turned my car around and headed toward the Dwarf House, the original Chick-fil-a.

I texted back: On my way. Once inside the Dwarf House, we all hugged because we were one step away from justice. The next court date would be jury selection for the trial.

Norma was smiling ear to ear. She knew how close we were to getting justice for Melissa. Tina said, "Christopher was a no-show. Not even his girlfriend was there. No one was there for him."

She then said, "And guess what? The defense came over to the prosecution table and asked, 'What's the plea offer?' And the prosecutor looked and him and said, 'There's no deal. It's life.'"

Norma said, "That's right, no deal!"

Tina added, "I've said from day one. No deal."

Chapter 38

THE JURY HAS SPOKEN

NORMA TEXTED AT 10:49 AM on May 22, 2025. She is headed downtown for court prep. She is happy that Adrian will be there. I am too. When you have a trusted, devoted, and capable prosecutor it feels different going through the system. It's not as scary for families and witnesses. Testifying is not easy for veteran officers with training and experience. For someone who has little to no experience it can be intimidating and frustrating. For Norma the last time she testified in open court she testified against Carl. Those can't be easy flashbacks and memories.

June 12, 2025, Norma and Tina stopped by my office to talk about the upcoming trial. They sat down in my new chairs laughing that my closet was getting highfalutin. We laughed because my office was the supply closet for the department until I transformed it into something that was my own. We talked about the trial and how close we were to having justice. We talked and laughed while reading over some of Carl's letters. Then we recalled their victim impact statements. Norma said she was lost, could not put into words what was taken from her. She took a moment and quietly and softly began to speak about when Melissa was just missing, then finding only her skull, the trash bags, the identification, the notification, and being left on the porch all alone. I said, there's your impact statement.

Karyn Greer and I met in Piedmont Park to tape an episode for her upcoming new segment. As we were laughing and talking and kinda working, the conversation turned to Melissa and her upcoming trial. Karyn said, "Have you heard Adrian has been pulled off again?" I literally took a step back and said, "No!" Karyn said Adrian had been reassigned to another rapper case. I was so disappointed for Norma and Tina. Once again their case was not as important as the glitz and glamour of a rapper's trial. Melissa was once again pushed aside. She will get second best if that. Sunday is Father's Day, their first one without Carl. I think I'll wait to tell them this news.

I have climbed these steps hundreds of times. As I ascend these steps for court today, I reflect on hearings, trials, testimonies, visiting friends but today feels different. Today is a moment that will be etched in stone. Like these granite steps, with its unyielding properties, it serves as a metaphor for the everlasting impact this case will have on me. This stone hosts legacy, like Mount Rushmore, the Vietnam Veterans Memorial in Washington, DC, and thousands of headstones. The timeless structure of this courthouse echoes the enduring quest for justice. The jury, these twelve strangers, have no idea the history, connections, and the overwhelming desire I have to see this case through to a conviction. This trial will be my last major case wearing a badge. I may be the only one who realizes this fact but it's true. Crazy to think someone else will be called 149. They may have to retire that number, honey. No one can live up to "Shirley," "Seven," or "Mac Attack." I have found myself in deep reflection and gratitude for this career over the past several months. For all of the people who paved the way, held the door open, kept the light on, and often handed me the keys, I pray I have done that for a few. As I think about Huck and Caroline starting their careers, I know they are starting ahead of the curve because they have some significant people in their phone. People who will guide, support, and cheer them on.

I'm in the elevator now. I joined a group of defense attorneys and a young officer. One of the attorneys I recognized immediately. We exchanged hellos and then asked what brought us here today. The officer looks about twenty-five years old. He was busy on his phone. He never looked up and never spoke. I wished I could tell him to talk to these men, "Hell, talk to me!" There's over a hundred years of experience in this elevator. Start adding folks to your Rolodex. Oh well, the doors opened and he got off. My floor is next and I wrap up my conversation with the old guard and turn right toward the courtroom. I find myself scanning for Norma and Tina. I can't imagine how they are feeling. They have been subpoenaed so they can't be in the courtroom. The defense subpoenaed me. I will stay clear and go to Adrian's office.

Friday is closing arguments. My sister Sharlene goes to court with me. The defense never called me. They mentioned my name over and over but never called me as a witness. I speak to the deputy guarding the courtroom door. Christopher is in a wheelchair. I can't help but think about Carl. He would steal a phone today for sure. Not borrow or barter, but steal. He would be on pins and needles for an update every day.

The verdict is in. The family has been summoned to the courthouse.

The jury foreman stands—"In the matter of the State of Georgia versus Christopher Wolfenbarger…not guilty."

The jury has spoken. Christopher Wolfenbarger was found not guilty. I will accept this verdict. I stand by the evidence seen and unseen by this jury. I stand by the work and efforts put forth by the police, district attorney, Melissa's family, and our team. My buddy and mentor, John B. Edwards texted me:

> Remember circumstantial cases are always tough.
> Especially when they rely on testimonial evidence.

He is right. This case did not offer the jury solid evidence like DNA, fingerprints, or an eyewitness. The case fell short. After twenty-seven years some evidence is just not there for this jury.

There are some folks the jury did not hear from: me. Why would the defense send me a subpoena and never call me to the stand? But they said my name over and over and over, where I worked, and the name of my podcast. Then there is the Fayette County detective who went and met with Carl about searching for Melissa. Why not call him to the stand and let him explain that Carl had nothing to do with Melissa's murder but in fact wanted it solved? How about the female detective in Henry County who told Melissa, "If you don't get away from him, he's going to kill you"? The state never called Francine Bardole, the DNA expert. Remember it came out in trial that Christopher said he "knew how to kill someone and get away with it," that he knew "where to hide a body." If you are still not convinced, remember Christopher confessed. The jury never heard about it but he confessed to his mother's preacher.

The sun came up, the Flint still runs, and we will fight another day. There are other victims and families who need our induvial and collective help. Norma was hurt and a little broken over the verdict. She sought the comfort of her preacher and family. Tina was angry and will use this experience to fight domestic violence through education and maybe even create an organization in her sister's name.

As for me, the jury came back Friday and I was back on duty Monday at 7:00 a.m. My daughter Caroline said, "This means no matter who you believe killed Melissa—a killer got away with it." She's right. No one disagrees that Melissa was murdered in a horrific manner and left like trash in a junk yard. And no one will ever pay the price for killing her. My son Huck said, "This is your *To Kill A Mockingbird*, use it." He's right.

The bald cypress is the classic tree of southern rivers and swamps that stand over a hundred feet tall. They have these crazy roots that grow vertically, called "knees" rising up from the water around the base of the tree. These trees are native to the Flint. It's amazing to think these trees are standing in water. These roots stabilize the soil and provide stability for these giants. So, even a river has help! And I have had a lot of it.

The irony of the new thirty-one-mile trail network that will connect Atlanta, East Point, College Park, and Hapeville to the long-overlooked Flint River is not lost on me. Atlanta where I was born, East Point where I grew up, College Park where I went to school, and Hapeville where I work and where I worked to solve Melissa's case will all forever be connected.

The Flint will be unearthed just like the truth in this case and Carl's cases. People don't know they are passing a river, just like in Melissa's case they did not know they were passing her body parts. Her murder was hidden. The Atlanta Police did not even know she was a missing person much less a homicide victim even though she lay right there for years waiting to be discovered. And in Carl's crimes he used the hidden waters of Flint to hide his crimes.

I want to speak directly to you. To thank you for reading Melissa's story. I hope this case inspires you to action. Whether you are in law enforcement or a civilian you can help solve a cold case. Look at all the civilians who helped on Melissa's case. Like the cypress, you can help the river of unsolved cases. There are thousands of missing persons cases and cold case homicides that need your help. When I think about all the cases sitting on shelves in boxes and all the talent sitting out there unused, I get inspired to connect people with cases. I want to get the right case, at the right time, to the right people.

The Flint begins near my hometown in a small, wooded area, where it's either obscured by culverts, or down the road hidden beneath runways, or fenced-off on airport property. Cold cases often have evidence obscured, hidden, or fenced off figuratively and literally. Once you locate the headwaters the larger parts can be mapped out. This can be done in reverse. If you are standing at the large open water of the Flint you can traverse backwards until the headwaters are located. I work cold cases backwards. I start at the ending, where the victim was found deceased. I work backwards the last twenty-four hours of their life. This leads me to the start of the murder. I had to go back to the Flint. The place where I played cops and robbers. To see this hidden land of my childhood before it becomes an open place for citizens and visitors to enjoy. As I feel the perpetual motion of retirement is coming at me fast I realize I have many things to pass along to the next generation. This hidden place will no longer be a secret, it will be soon be exposed and open to everyone. But today I will once again hide here and have it all to myself. I will sit by this magical fountain and enjoy the quiet reflection of a career I am proud of. I am no longer pretending there are bandits to catch. I have done what few have had the privilege of doing and that is living my childhood dream.

Melissa's case fell short of justice but there's still a lot we can do. Carl and I were unlikely partners. We worked together to try and see justice served. We were an odd pairing but found common ground. That's a bigger life lesson. Some days we were just two parents. I know he did some terrible things to some innocent people, but Melissa did not deserve what happened to her. Carl suffered for his crimes. Carl deserved to be in prison for the rest of his life. But he still deserved justice for his child. I felt it fitting that Carl had the last word. He would often tell friends, his children, and me, if work, family, or the world gets tough or overwhelming—"Why aren't you doing something!"

Final Thought from a Friend

THERE ARE THOSE THAT STAND on the sidelines and watch. Or they sit comfortably in their seats and...observe. Their hands never get dirty, they never take a hit, they never get bloody or sweaty, and they never, ever lose.

They never lose because they don't dare to struggle, to enter the fray and do what they must to endure until the bitter end.

They also never win.

Sheryl McCollum joined me in the good fight many years ago and she never left. We fought and continue to fight for what is justice in our world.

She follows the case where it takes her, to the good, and sometimes, the bad. Yes, we know we may lose in the end, or we may win. We may get justice or walk out of the courtroom empty handed. But she could never live with herself if she didn't follow every lead, run with it, and be ready to get in the ring, on the field, in the thick of it.

She is a modern-day gladiator. I am proud we have fought, and continue to fight, so many battles together.

Nancy Grace

Appendix

Monday

Ms Sheryl, Sept 2, 2024

Greeting once again from paradice (my donkey). As you can tell I hate this place more with each passing day. Mostly because I get no Atlanta news and can't keep up with how Melissa's case is going. I need to be moved north and closer to Atlanta. You, Norma and Tina Mae do your best, but it's not the same having to wait 2 or 3 days. If, you understand my meaning?

You said in your last letter you had the ending for the book; I disagree! The verdict, has not came yet and the sentence has not been passed yet. Can you tell me anything about the judge? I know it is a woman and I hope that means toughness and not a bunny hugger! What about the Lawyer? Who is he or she? Is he tough enough to get Chris freed? Will there be a bond set? If, he gets bond, he will run! I am worried about Joey. Chris has had 20 yrs or more to brain-wash him with lies. Christina knows the truth, how I do not know but, if she sees through the lies why can't Joey? Cathy and Kimberly both know the truth also, and have said they knew as soon as Melissa disappeared, but you'll never get either one to admit it. Both are liars also!

as for the writtings I am doing about my past crimes, people and places assciated with such, I'm along way from complettion. If I do complete it, not sure I want it read. It's mostly self-therapy and self-awareness that my God has walked with me for a very long time. I have cheated death three time in my life: No one cheats death unless God helps you. Let lone 3 times! Maybe one day when we meet I'll tell you!

Couple other things, the news people from Canada, and Mark Winnie want to make all this news coverage about me not Melissa. As you know, I said from the start it's about Melissa and getting her justice. The Canadian people tricked Norma, and I am very upset about it! Plus, I have no clue where Mark Winnie comes in thinking he's gona step on Ms Green's feet and take over. I told Mark Winnie 21½ years ago, I do nothing for free he said he could not pay for an interview, end of story! To me he's a back-stabber, bottom feeder and as long as I have anything to say about him getting an interview: Never happen!

Two of the prayers I have been asking for, for over 15 years was answered this past month. First was the killed would be named and brought to the public's eye, Second God would let me live to see it. My third is for me to get home, become a member of Phillippi Baptist Church, to help my family heal from the pain and hardship Chris and I have caused. Two out of three so far and the third is closer than anyone thinks! When I called the dinner I knew I forgot to thank someone, please convey my thanks to everyone!

As for Walt, Norma said you and he are a team like she and I, couldn't leave him out. Norma says he does real good reading my words, thank you Walt! Thank you Ms Sheryl for the picture and frame you gave Norma, means alot to know you care!

Thank you for the (Mug shot) look at it most nights before I go to sleep! Really helps knowing he's in jail, too!

Hope to see you sooner than later!

Carl
2024

Ms Sheryl!
Sorry it took so long to answer your letter, have been in quarantine due to the flu, it took more than a week for mail to catch up to me. The last letter had afew more questions, which I'll try to answer.

1 Norma's loyalty: Would expect nothing less from my Soul mate, we grew up togeather and we're joined at the hip. I Knew what she's gona do in any situation and she can answer any question someone may ask me. In other Words we are one.

2 Was I scared about starting my own business? No, I'm good at my craft, and if I told someone I'd do it I did, Plus the one that taught me said, I always had a job waitting whenever I needed it.

3. Why did we ask Jordan to find Melissa, that was Norma, no one in Fulton Co was doing anything, although Melissa's body was in the Fulton Co morgue nearly 5 years. So when Jordan wanted Norma to testify aginst me she made a deal, he'd find Melissa and she'd testify.

4 How do I feel about Jordan? He's a manipulating lieing, S.O.B, he and I had a deal too, he'd leave my family alone and I'd plead guilty. I done my part, but, they still gave Norma 1 year probation and $1,000 fine, plus he was gona

get Chris, Well, we Know he didn't get Chris! But, on the other hand he did find Melissa which did get her case attention. He did his job by getting me, I'd like to Know what he did to get fired.

5 How is God helping now to bring justice for Melissa? Three words: Sheryl Mc, D.A. Love, Det Stein, and I am grateful everyday for you, three!

6 Where do I feel the most at peace? That is in the visitation room whenever Norma comes to visit. The only time I feel whole is when I can hold my wife and feel her embrace. The rest of the time I feel like I don't count, that probably comes from living in a warehouse, and Know the World and time is passing me by.

If, it sounds like I'm giving up, I'm not. I do believe one day the board will let me go home to my family. I just hope they don't wait till I'm a burden on my family or need a wheelchair to get around.

Loneliness and depression sometimes sneak up on me, but I try to stay possitive! Please Keep me informed on any movement. Thank you for all you've done already!

Later

Carl

2022

Ms Sheryl! Oct 11 2022.

Congratulations on your upcoming Pod-cast, will be looking forward to listening. Being's you'll be under Nancy's umbrella it should go national with lots more exposeure. Well also be looking forward to hearing Norma and Tina Mae speak about Melissa's case. My wife is a very smart lady; she's still working to change me from a lump of coal to a dimond, Ha! Ha! On our last visit, I mentioned that if I had to forgive to be forgiven then I'd burn in hell, cause I'll never forgive Chris for what he's done to our family. That next week she sent me this, "So often we have trouble letting go of an offence because we think that means we are ignoring it or accepting the wrong. But, that is not what forgiveness is or means, Instead it means we are looking to the Lord to make it right on our behalf," So the Lord will Take care of it in his own time."

The Cherokee and Cheyenne say when you kill something whether animal or human it becomes apart of you forever and that you never forget. I personally know this to be True, after over 45 years I still remember my actions and sins. Do you think Chris Wolfenburger ever thinks about the mutilation done to Melissa's body?

How do you kill the mother of your two children, then look those children in the eye and say your mother deserted you because she didn't want you? Then when it's proven their mother is dead, and they want to visit the grave, you take em to a different location and claim someone must have moved her.

Ms Sheryl, I have told you, I had to loose Melissa and feel the pain to really realize the damage and harm I caused people I did not know. Please tell me who does Chris have to loose to realize the hurt, heart break and anguish his actions caused? A guilty conscience is a hell on Earth that continues to punish and convict, and I deal with it everyday. I pray that one day soon Chris will get a conscience and see the wrong he has done. To face the man in the mirror is a continuous struggle that I face everyday. If, I could talk to the Parole Board members I'd tell em their not doing anything to me I haven't already done, their not punishing me, now theyre punishing my family.

Cathy Wolfenburger is guilty of concealing a crime, she has known all along what Chris had done, if not why did she tell Chris he needed to talk to the Preacher? So please find something big or small to charge her with!

I wish Chris had Killed me instead of Melissa, that way I wouldn't have to live with the guilt of Knowing I was not there to protect her, everytime I look at her picture. Pain is the price you pay for loving your children so deeply.

I told Chris on more than one occation, if he ever got tired of her to call us and we'd come get her. He did not have to Kill her, and for the life of me I can not understand why.

Ms Sheryl, Norma, my family and myself has put alot of faith in you getting the truth and giving us real closure. Norma says she Knows why, but I think it's deeper than what we think. Once again thank you for your efforts in Melissa case. You're a God sent and we'll never be able to thank you enough or repay your Kindness!

God Bless you,

Carl
2022

Ms Sheryl,

Thank you for taking time out of your busy Scheduale to write and continue to Keep me informed on Melissa's case. Last week was a rough one, Melissa would have turned 45 on Friday. Your letters are greatly appreciated, they continue to re-asure me that someone other than family is concerned and seeking justice for her. Thank you for your efforts and determanation on Melissa's behalf. My family and I owe you a debt of graditude that can not be repaid.

Norma was here Saturday for our visit. She told me that D.N.A was retrieved from the bags, now they have to match everything togeather. My hopes continue to grow, but sounds like the walls are closing in on the Killer! Norma also told me Chris and Cathy were saying I Killed Melissa to frame Chris, Ms Sheryl we both Know there's no way I'd ever hurt one of my children, but: If that ever comes up in your presence; ask what did chris do to make me hate him enough to Kill my baby girl? The reason I hate his ass, is because he Killed my daughter. He and his mother are bigger fools than I thought. That statement proves it!

In your letter you mentioned Norma and Tina Mae going to crimecon next year when you present Melissa's case, I think that would be awsome, but, we do need closure. So Melissa's story will show, there is no perfect murder or crime, and that no matter how long it takes, answers and truth will come to light.

Trying to peice things togeather, to start writting my life story, from childhood up to now. Want to show life experiences that made me the way I was, and how I've changed to the person I am now. Any names I mention would be protected by statue of limitations or they are dead and gone. Will not change names to protect the innocent, because there where no innocent!

Appreciate your enthusiasm on the parol board changing their minds about me. Don't see it happening. They group all inmates togeather and we never change, no matter what. God forgive the board doesn't. They only look at what you done 20,30,45 years ago, not what you are today. But, thanks for the wishful thinking. They're hurting my family now!

Sincerly
Carl
2022

P.S. (Lock Chris up please) (over)

Me and my family need to see Chris on national News! Please get his ass.
"Thank You"

Ms Sheryl, July 22, 2021

Once again, thank you for your efforts in Melissa's case, My family and myself will never be able to repay your Kindness and exchange of thoughts in our quest for Justice We all Know who done the crime now it's time he does the time. Forgive me for asking but what's taking so long? Please excuse my impatience, but we have been waiting 20 years now! Bless ADA Lowe in her efforts also, You and I both Know a D.A. can get a verdict of guilty with much less than she has on Chris. I'm sure she Knows what she's doing and I mean no disrespect in anyway, I'm Just a hurting Father that has waited too long!

In reguard to your letter, dated 7-1-2021. I have spoken with Norma and Tina Mae, For you an officer of the courts with your reputation and qualifications in the field of criminal behavior, would be a game changer for me in front of the Parole Board, and I promise I won't disappoint you or embarrass you in anyway!

I want the producer of 20/20 to move forward Still feel I don't need to appear, but will give a statement to be aired on their program Have a list of questions I'd like ask also.

Melissa Dawn was my baby girl, who owned my heart, first time I held her. She was a happy beautiful young lady. Made good grades in school was in R.O.T.C and had a bright future in front of her. All that changed when she met Chris Wolfenburger. He had an unhealty influence on her. She changed and not for the better; She started sneaking out at night to meet him and do (God Knows what) He even talked her into stealing my car. (Twice) She and Chris had planned to run away to California! (His idea) After Melissa became pregnant and had Christina, Chris done everything he could to Keep Melissa and Christina away from Me and Norma, Now she had to sneak away from him, not sneak to meet him! Only time we got to see Melissa and Christina was when Chris was at work. Melissa told us she'd be in big trouble if he found out! She often had bruises on her arms and neck! Norma and I tried to tell her it was an unsafe and unhealty relationship but, she was in love and wouldn't listen.

When Melissa didn't show up at Christmas to get her gifts and then we couldn't locate her, I knew in my mind and heart Chris had done something to Melissa. Never thought it was this bad. When we went to their address and everything was gone, no one knew where they had gone, then I really Knew something had had happened. Melissa Dawn would never leave her children, as Chris has claimed over the years. Plus she would call her mother and sister if possible!

"My statement to 20/20 is as follows"

My name is Carl Patton, I'm Melissa Dawn Patton Wolfenbargers Father. I'm currently housed in Dodge State Prison. I want anyone and everyone who reads or hears this to Know, there is no excuss for what I done as a young man in 1977 and as an ole man in 2021 I am ashame, remorseful and very sorry for my actions. I had no idea the harm I caused not only to my victims but also their families and friends, but once we lost Melissa it came very clear I was wrong and misguided in the actions I took, and had caused great harm to individuals I didn't Know. May God forgive me.

Unlike the person that Killed Melissa Dawn I have taken reponsibility and accepted my punisement. It is time for Melissa Killer to do the same. No more lies, No more running, No more hiding, stand up and be a man, tell the truth. If not for your own conscious then for the health and well being of your children. They deserve to Know what really happened to their mother and why. There is only one suspect they are coming for you! Forgiveness aways starts with confession!!!

(over)

Ms Sheryl.

If, possible, when you arrest Chris Wolfenbarger
be sure he gets as much publicity as I
did! If, not more!

Thank you

Carl

2021

"Questions to Chris on 20/20" (From Carl Patton)

(1) If, you had nothing to do with Melissa's disappearance & Murder, Why didn't you call the police or her parents when you couldn't locate her?

(2) Why did you move to Dublin and not contact anyone?

(3) Why when Bruce Jordan came to Dublin with a warrant for your D.N.A. Did you grab warrant and run?

(4) Why haven't you tried to help find your wife?

(5) Why was the house you and Melissa lived in at time of her disappearance gutted and redone soon after her disappearance and your move to Dublin

(6) Why does your Daughter who was 2½-3 years old at time, say you killed her mother?

(7) Why did you lie to Christina & Joey about the location of where their mother grave was?

(8) Why have you and your family always lied about Melissa leaving on her own?

(9) Why have you and your family always Kept Christina and Joey away from Melissa's parents, to the point of keeping Chrismas and birthday cards sent to them from Melissa parents?

(10) Why did you and your family always tell Christina & Joey their mothers Parents wanted nothing to do with em?

(11) Why was it so importent for you and your mother to have custody of Christina and Joey, when at one time you both let her live in car on streets homeless?

(12) (Personal Question) from Carl Patton to Chris, do you really think you're smart enough to get away with murder?

(13)

What type man, has a young pretty wife, who loved him, would do anything for him legal or otherwise, who gave him two beautiful children and was probably pregnant with 3rd. Kill her and cut her up and put her in garbage bags and through her away like trash? Just) a Hypothetical question I'd like someone to answer!

(14) Can you explain why Melissa's body parts were found so close to your address) and her torse is still missing?

(15) If, she was found were she was killed and dismember, Why would the Killer take time to put her body parts in plastic bags?

In The Superior **Court Of** Fulton **County**

State Of Georgia

TO: Sheryl McCollum

SUBPOENA FOR THE PRODUCTION OF EVIDENCE

You are hereby required to be and appear at the Fulton County Superior Court before Rachel R. Krause, Judge of Superior Court in Courtroom 4B of the Fulton County Courthouse, 136 Pryor St., Atlanta, GA at 9:30 a.m. on August 12, 2025,and to bring with you into said Court certain documents to be used as evidence by Defendant in a certain case pending in said Court between State of Georgia and Christopher Wolfenbarger, Case no. 24SC004201.

The following are hereby subpoenaed:

All personal correspondence between you and Carl Millard Patton, Jr. (including, but not limited to, all letters referenced on the "Zone 7" podcast, "Letters from Carl Patton," March 15, 2023, and any responses from you or your colleagues or staff to him) which may in any way pertain to Melissa Wolfenbarger or Christopher Wolfenbarger

In advance of your personal appearance, please send by mail, hand delivery, or email to jm@gsllaw.com, fair and accurate copies of said property to Attorney Joel McDurmon or direct staff, at 3151 Maple Dr NE, Atlanta, GA 30305, on or before August 8, 2025.

Herein fail not, under penalty of law.

Witness Rachel R. Krause Judge of said Court this August 4, 2025.

Any Questions Contact:
Joel E. McDurmon, Esq.
Garland, Samuel & Loeb, P.C.
3151 Maple Dr., N.E.
Atlanta, Georgia 30305
Phone: 404-262-2225
Email: jm@gsllaw.com

Ché Alexander,
Clerk of Superior Court
404-613-5314

Subpoena Issued by Attorney of Record for Defendant

RETURN OF SERVICE

I served the within witness ___________________ with this subpoena on ___________ at _______ am/pm by: ____ delivering to him/her in person, or by ____ registered or certified mail.

Served by: ______________________________
Name and Title

"Pursuant to OCGA 24-13-21(c-h), this subpoena form is being provided to the attorney of record and shall be completed prior to service upon the witness. If an individual misuses a subpoena, he or she shall be subject to punishment for contempt of court and shall be punished by a fine of not more than $300.00 or not more than 20 days imprisonment, or both. A witness may contact the Clerk of Court's office to verify this subpoena was issued for a valid case."

SC-9 (modified for issuance by attorney)
Rev'd 1/25

IN THE SUPERIOR COURT OF Fulton COUNTY
STATE OF GEORGIA

TO: Sheryl McCollum
[Witness name]

[Witness address]

WITNESS SUBPOENA

THE COURT DIRECTS YOU to lay all other business aside to appear to testify in Courtroom 4B of the Fulton County Courthouse, 136 Pryor St SW, Atlanta, GA 30303 [address] at 9:30 o'clock ☒ A.M. or ☐ P.M. on August 12, 2025 [date of appearance] to be sworn as a witness for the Defense in the case of State of Georgia vs. Wolfenbarger Case no. 24SC004201.

The court requires you to attend from day to day and from time to time until the case is disposed of.

HEREIN FAIL NOT, under the authority of Rachel Krause Judge of said Court this 4 day of August, 2025.

Che' Alexander
Clerk of Superior Court
Fulton County, Georgia

If you have questions, contact:
Joel E. McDurmon, Esq. (attorney for Defendant)
Phone: 678-772-0790
Email: jm@gsllaw.com

SC-8
Rev'd 10/24

Garland, Samuel & Loeb, P.C.
TRIAL ATTORNEYS

3151 Maple Drive, N.E.
Atlanta, Georgia 30305
Telephone (404) 262-2225
Facsimile (404) 365-5041
www.gsllaw.com

Edward T. M. Garland
Donald F. Samuel
Robin N. Loeb
John A. Garland
Amanda Clark Palmer
Kristen W. Novay
Joel E. McDurmon

Reuben A. Garland (1903-1982)

August 4, 2025

Dear Witness,

Please call me at 678-772-0790 to discuss the enclosed subpoena. Our discussion may preclude the need for you to testify, and I may be able to release you from the subpoena.

Sincerely,

/s/ Joel McDurmon
JOEL E. MCDURMON
Georgia Bar No. 902163

Acknowledgments

Tina

Junior! Keep that family loyalty. You are the glue. You fought and saw this case through. Like Carl told me, "We are family now!"

Norma

You fought like only a momma could. You knew Melissa was in danger first. You knew first something was terribly wrong. And you made sure her case was going to get solved first!

Carl

I told you in my last letter to you what working with you on this case meant to me. It meant it got solved. I welcomed your skilled wording, crafty observation, and ultimately your insight into this killer.

My Zone 7 is filled with brilliant, caring, generous and kind people. Here are just a few who I must publicly thank:

Dr. Angie Arnold

What a ride, Doc! You provided your expertise at a Wine & Crime. Were a phone call away when I had a question or needed to understand part of the psychology of this crime. You were such a gift to Tina. Most people have no idea the 361 that was done on this case by so many thoughtful and caring experts. You paid attention to the most important person who needed help. You also threw an amazing dinner party at the country club so that we could all celebrate the arrest of Melissa's killer.

Donna Jones Llanes

We would not be here if not for you. Tina meeting you and talking about her sister started this whole chain of events. You telling her she had to meet your friend from high school and her running with that—man, who would have ever thought this would be the result—a conviction! Thank you for your love and friendship over the years!

Dr. Trace Sargent

You are never farther than a phone call. What a comfort. We have worked on many cold cases including a Dixie Mafia case, missing persons, homicides, but this case I saw up close your advocacy for the families. It is always an incredible experience working with you and your amazing K9s. You did not hesitate once again to show up and work your dogs in an effort to give the family answers. You are one of my go-to folks.

Susan Hendricks

You were the first person I showed this book to. You are a dear friend and confidant. You were so supportive and kind about the pitiful rough draft. Knowing I can't spell did not deter you from giving me such kind and supportive feedback. You offered to read as I wrote, to edit, to call your manager and publisher. What a generous and sweet friend you are.

Karyn Greer

There are no words to describe how much your friendship and partnership mean to me. For over twenty years I have relied on your guidance and leadership. You have never once betrayed my trust. You have kept this case alive for twenty years. You at times have been the only person covering this story. Thank you for allowing me to tag along.

DA Fani Willis

Thank you for meeting with me before you even took office and letting me lay out five cases that I believed could be solved by your office. Your leadership in assigning ADA Love to this case was a needed move. That lit a fire under this case. We have almost solved all five! Thank you for the confidence in putting me on your Cold Case Task Force and the SAKI Task Force and letting me work on these important cases.

Kevin Balfe

What support and stellar collaboration. CrimeCon has transformed my career. You and the CC Team have made certain that I have been able to showcase many of our cases. Having a national stage can absolutely help solve a cold case and has. We have had numerous cases from CrimeCon moved forward or solved by your backing. Natalie Wood, death certificate changed to undetermined. Nacole Smith, solved. Natalie Holliway, solved. Kate Arquite, solved. Honey Malone, solved. And now Melissa Wolfenbarger. This book only happened because of your connections. Thank you!

Leslie Saunders

Bay! You are not only my best partner but my best friend. We have literally worked every major crime together. There has never been a mass event that I did not feel completely at ease when I looked over at you. Even the active scene with bullets still flying you could make me laugh. The Adamsville Slaying, the Olympic Park bombing, the Oklahoma City bombing, the Boston Strangler case, 9/11 the Pentagon, the courthouse shootings, and many, many more. It's not just professional where you show up. You have been right there for over thirty years. We are family.

Francine Bardole

Your invention of the Bardole Method of extracting DNA from small items was a game changer. You have helped me on numerous cold cases, finding answers and suspects. On this case you were critical. We had to test the trash bags and see if it lead to our killer. No one else could have been more caring and intelligent about how we proceeded. You have without a doubt become a dear friend over the years. Thank you for the friendship and expertise.

Dr. Duanne Thompson

My buddy. We have had some wild times, searching rivers, climbing over live electric fence, serial killer hunting, clandestine graves, animal poaching, bombings, courthouse shootings, and catching a killer using a killer. Your friendship is one of my most valued. Your help on Melissa's case was vital. You searched for the saw. You graphed the victimology and suspectology. You were fantastic with law enforcement and the family. Thank you for always being there.

Nancy Grace

I have the career I have today because of you! You have made me a better investigator in every way. Under your leadership I learned the importance of doing it right. No shortcuts. Every case is equally as important as the next. You always approached major cases as a team. Pull in everyone. Work it from all sides. Do what you know to be the right thing. Never let your foot off the gas. An arrest does not stop the investigation. Write a good report. You will testify based on what you wrote, not what you did. Go where the case leads you! You put this case on the national map. You gave Melissa a voice that reached millions. Her family was knocked out by your efforts and willingness to help. You know how much I rely on your guidance and case assessment. Your advice is the title of this book. *Swans Don't Swim in A Sewer*! You have been my dear friend for over forty years! I love, adore, and admire you! I'm riding them coattails.

Dr. Joni Johnston

Your brilliance and easy natural way of making the world better is such a talent. Your steady advice and sweet friendship has been a source of comfort over the years. The day we spent talking about this case and looking at the file at the lake was not only a stunning backdrop, it was a much needed retreat. You gave me clarity on the way we were working and how to best present the circumcisional evidence. Thank you for your friendship and the adventures!

DDA Adrian Love

That first day we met it was electrifying in that I knew from the first second things were going to happen on several cold cases. You had the drive, intellect, and the position to get things done! I remember calling Norma and telling her you were the answer.

Joe Scott Morgan

I can hear Norma right now, "Do you think Joe Scott Morgan will look at Melissa's case? I just think the world of him." You not only provided brilliant assessments of what happened to Melissa but you provided comfort and genuine friendship to her family. The Wine & Crime, autopsy review, case assessment, and overall action plan. Norma, Tina, and Carl gained so much through your care and advocacy. You know I love and respect you and your life's work. You have added greatly to my professional and private life. Bon ami—family.

Captain Nicole Brock

Brock! Baby, we have had some great times. We have worked some fascinating and scary scenes. I always love the way you put people first. You are slow to react to negativity but fast to respond to positivity. Your talks and evaluation of Melissa's case were solid. I often tell rookies, "Who cares what I think?" I have so many experts that I draw from and collectively that is a massive statement. I adore you and can't wait for our next "happening" as you say!

Sgt. Layton

We were all thrilled when you joined us for the CrimeCon in house conference and helped us present Melissa's case. This was during COVID when no one could leave their homes to attend large events and conferences. You provided such a clear and deliberate lock on the case. People understood in that moment that the Atlanta Police Department did not care that over twenty years had passed, y'all were coming for this killer. Your steady leadership over the homicide unit was remarkable. With so many gifted and determined detectives this case was set to see an arrest. Thank you for your alliance over the years.

Detective Shephard

You got the darn thing done! You were so willing to take phone calls, tips, and connectivity information. Your kindness toward Carl was impressive. I will never forget the phone call Carl made during our celebration dinner and how respectful you were. Congratulations on the arrest and conviction.

John Arnold Jr.

I will never forget our meeting at the club. I felt like Elvis! Your generous support has been a constant baseline for me. Your quick friendship and ready advice have shaped this book.

Leigh Egan

There has not been one event or story you have not covered for the CCIRI. Melissa's was no different. Because of the national spotlight that you helped cultivate we were able to keep the attention on this case. I appreciate your willingness to help keep these cold cases alive and the answers coming!

Betsy Ramsey

Your council and advice has been my rock for thirty years. You have never once led me wrong. I appreciate the love and friendship over the years. The advice and steadfast guidance have been the foundation of every case.

Stephanie Scott Synder

Having your expertise as well as your students proved to have a solid impact on this case. We knew we were on the right track, but having such a diverse and brilliant set of eyes was a gift. I rely on the fact that you will jump on a plane anytime to help! Thank you for your friendship and clear advice.

Kelly McLear

Talk about national attention on a case. You not only made sure this case was in the spotlight but did it during COVID when everything was shut down. You then put this case in CrimeHQ as well as CrimeCon. Thousands of people saw the case from a standpoint like no other—the victim's mother who also helped a killer.

Meliss Swindell

You have given us such a platform to showcase these important cases. The Georgia Writers Museum has set the standard in advocacy and fundraising for these cases to have evidence tested, experts brought in, and to have the general public offer support and assistance. Thank you for your tireless efforts on every case.

Douglas MacGregor

What a gift you have. Not just in your area of expertise but your fast action to help. You have a drop everything and assist in real time attitude. In Melissa's case, because of you we had something new that law enforcement did not previously have on her case—crime mapping. You and I had never met and from another country you gave every effort to help show who the killer was.

Sgt. Joe Giacalone

Never has a call to you gone unanswered. Not once. You have offered your genius many times on cases, but Melissa's was particularly Sarg'esque. Straightforward, funny, and correct. Thank you for your humor and direction over the years. Your friendship and established comradery have meant the world.

Detective Calhoun

Parent to parent, your leadership on this case set the standard. Your thoughtfulness, consideration, and compassion were the bar. Every officer, prosecutor, CSI, and detective should strive to see the world like you do. Carl was a parent first in your eyes. I hope this book does your kind-heartedness justice.

Laura Ingle

Thank you for the selfless act of giving this story away to an anchor. You believed this story was more important than the "scoop." You consistently demonstrate the level of competence and skill that only comes from a real pro. To me that is that people come first. Not the headline or the get, but the people. You are a generous and loving friend who gives more than most. Melissa's story was important to you and therefore important to others—thank you. I can't wait to walk a scene with you again!

Lauren Colin

Street level advocacy and storytelling. You know everyone. You are a true friend to everyone. You are a gracious and kind reporter who sees the world through your faith. You are quick to connect with others, which only proves your generosity. All our talks include laughter and our stories about our families. Laughing and family ties are a great way to go through this world. I appreciate our friendship.

Wilson Garrett

The consistency in your leadership and guidance has been unyielding. *Zone 7* would not exist if not for you. I rely on your friendship as much as your wisdom.

Alice LaCour

Your honest and supportive review made all the difference in the book getting ink to paper. There is nothing more comforting than having a friend you admire, adore, and trust. Thank you for sharing all your gifts with me.

Vic and Carolyn

Everything I am, is because of you.

The Wedge

Sharon, Sheila, Sharlene, Shelley, my original Zone 7. Y'all have never failed to support, advise, help, protect, aid, or nurture. When I no longer had parents y'all stepped up and stepped in. Everything I have ever done y'all have been right there improving it and making it better. In all ways—always.

Walt

I have loved you since I was fourteen. What a lucky girl to walk into detention late and have that sweet boy smile at me with an open seat beside him. Little did we know how that day would change our lives! You loved my parents, love my sisters, and love our children with every action possible.

Huck and Caroline

You are my whole world. Y'all have been to every major crime scene and met every expert, victim, family member, and criminal that I have worked with since 2000. What a gift to travel and experience this career with you. Y'all have added to this investigation, my career, and life beyond measure.

Joshua Schiffer

You told me once: "I really like complementing people as the recognition. Tell them that they have been very good at something, which is the basis for something else. Make a compound and multi clause"! When I asked for help, my friend you gave me solid and quick advice. I listened, now I am forever grateful!

Emily Huxford Pritchett and Jimmy Pritchett

With y'all there is no "our family" and "their family"—we are all family! Thank you for treating me like your own since I was fourteen.

About the Author

SHERYL "MAC" MCCOLLUM IS AN active crime scene investigator for a Metro Atlanta Police Department, and the director of the Cold Case Investigative Research Institute which collaborates with colleges and universities in the United States. She has worked on thousands of cold cases focusing on solvability factors with an investigative system she developed called the Last 24/361. This method utilizes the media, evidence, innovative forensic testing, and nationally recognized experts. Sheryl has been involved with some high profile and notable cases such as The Boston Strangler, Natalee Holloway, Tupac Shakur, and the Moore's Ford Bridge Lynching. This work earned her an Emmy on CSI: Atlanta. Sheryl is also the host of the cold case and investigative podcast *Zone 7. Sheryl has received many awards and commendations over her forty-four year career, but the pinnacle was when she was inducted into the National Law Enforcement Officer Hall of Fame in 2023.*